MASTERING
KNIFE SKILLS

MASTERING
KNIFE SKILLS

The Essential Guide to the Most Important Tools in Your Kitchen

Norman Weinstein

Photographs by Mark Thomas

STEWART, TABORI & CHANG - NEW YORK

Published in 2008 by Stewart, Tabori & Chang
An imprint of ABRAMS

Library of Congress Cataloging-in-
Publication Data

Weinstein, Norman.
  Mastering knife skills : the essential guide to
the most important tools in your kitchen / By
Norman Weinstein.
    p. cm.
  ISBN 978-1-58479-667-1
  1. Kitchen utensils. 2. Knives. I. Title.

TX656.G78 1986
643'.3—dc22

2007033419

Editor: Luisa Weiss
Designer: LeAnna Weller Smith
Production Manager: Tina Cameron

The text of this book was composed in
Benton Sans.

Printed and bound in Hong Kong
10 9 8 7 6 5

115 West 18th Street
New York, NY 10011
www.abramsbooks.com

FOR
CHI-CHI, MY WIFE, LIFE'S PARTNER, AND GUIDING LIGHT
AND
MY DEAR FRIENDS ANNA AMENDOLARA NURSE AND CAROLE WALTER,
WHO ENCOURAGED ME TO WRITE THIS BOOK—
MANY YEARS AGO

contents

introduction

Knife Skills, as a stand-alone course, was an offshoot of my many years as an instructor of Chinese cuisine. I realized my students needed to understand that the preparation of the ingredients was crucial to the outcome of the finished dish, that preparation often took more time than the actual cooking, and that good knife skills (actually cleaver skills, then) were essential to both Asian and Western cuisines.

Mastering Knife Skills thus represents the culmination of more than twenty-three years of thinking about, teaching, lecturing, and demonstrating this primary and essential skill in classrooms, lecture halls, and cookware stores. The inspiration to codify knife skills techniques came in great part from my students, first from analyzing the techniques they brought to the classroom, then thinking about how to solve the technical problems I witnessed in a way that could be easily communicated. It also came from the realization that the subject of knife skills is seriously neglected in cookbooks, food magazines, and cooking shows on television. Assumptions are made that the reader or viewer knows how to dice an onion or julienne a carrot. Those of us who teach cooking classes for the general public know full well that this assumption should never be made. The book is therefore devoted to filling this knowledge gap.

The popularity of and need for knife skills information can be attested to by the fact that in all the years I have been teaching, I have rarely had a class cancelled for lack of registration. Despite the fact that I currently teach over 120 classes a year at The Institute of Culinary Education in Manhattan, most are sold out. Some of my students have waited over a year to get in. I would like to attribute this wholly to my name and reputation, but I would be flattering myself. Students fill similar classes all over the country. They know that they need to learn this primary skill. Many of my students have admitted that the lack of good skills and the use of improper tools have made even simple meal preparation a grudging, time-consuming chore.

Mastering Knife Skills is designed to help the everyday household cook who, like it or not, has to put the daily bread on the table. By learning to select the proper knife and use it correctly with a maximum of ease and a minimum of stress, the preparation of the daily meal becomes a lot less time-consuming. I hope this book becomes your constant companion in the kitchen and that it expands not only your mechanical skills but your cooking repertoire as well.

PART I
A CONCISE HISTORY

CHAPTER ONE

From Stone to Steel

Imagine the consternation our distant ancestors must have experienced after the first mastodon was felled. Now what? Eighteenth-century Scottish biographer and diarist James Boswell characterized our species as a "cooking animal." But our ancestors' use of fire is believed to be only half as old as their use of cutting implements.

Sharpened stones would do the job at first. The discovery of metals and alloys would further refine this most basic survival tool, essential for hunting, fabricating (cutting into parts), eating, and even protection. The progression from primitive tool to modern kitchen knife in effect illustrates the history of metallurgy and modern engineering.

THE STONE AGE

It is estimated that mankind began making stone tools about two and a half million years ago. The earliest cutting tools were fashioned from flint (a form of silica), obsidian (a volcanic glass similar to granite), quartzite, or even jade, all fairly homogeneous materials that yield rather sharp edges if properly fashioned. These stones were, however, brittle and suitable only for short implements, usually no longer than 4 or 5 inches long. The essential commodities of hides and meat could be cut with stone tools, but it's unclear how durable the tools were.

Hard stones were used like a hammer to flake away bits of flint to achieve a point and sharp edges. No lathes, foundries, or fancy factories were required—the work space was simply a large rock or tree stump. Handles were fashioned from wood or bone, using a similar method. A short handle attached to a blade became a knife, a longer one indicated an axe, even longer, a spear. The shapes of many of our modern cutting tools bear an uncanny likeness to their Stone Age counterparts.

THE BRONZE AGE

The Bronze Age is not any one particular period but rather a stage of metallurgical advancement that occurred at different times in different parts of the world. The early Bronze Age is sometimes referred to as the Copper Age. Raw copper was pounded into tools as early as 10,000 B.C., but it proved too soft to make durable cutting tools. Bronze, an alloy made up of 85 to 95 percent copper most commonly mixed with tin, is harder than pure copper and melts at a lower temperature. Hard tools and weapons fashioned from bronze retained an edge far better than stone. So while very few implements of pure copper have been found, bronze knives have been discovered in great abundance in archeological digs all over Europe. Bronze artifacts, including knives, dating back to about 3000 B.C. have been found in the Near East, and recent discoveries indicate a Bronze Age in Thailand as far back as 4500 B.C.

>> Smiths of this period often added arsenic to the copper when smelting bronze because tin was not readily available in all regions. Though arsenic added durability, it also created toxic fumes; even when smiths learned to work outdoors, it was common for them to develop arsenic poisoning over a period of years. Much trial and error eventually led to the replacement of arsenic with tin as the other component of the alloy.

THE IRON AGE

The history of the modern knife begins not with the discovery of iron, but with the ability to smelt it and control its properties. That our modern knives are made from iron (to which carbon has been added to make steel) is a testament to our ancestors' ability to solve problems by trial and error—lots of error. Iron is much more difficult to smelt than copper. It requires a higher temperature and is actually still hard at the temperature at which copper melts. Iron contains impurities called slag. Some smith, perhaps out of extreme frustration, discovered that by hitting a lump of near-molten iron he was able to extract the slag. The resulting pure iron, known as wrought iron, is a soft iron that is carbon-free.

Introduce carbon into iron and the result is steel. The carbon came from the charcoal-fired forges in which the smelting was done—as a smith hammered away at the sword or plowshare he was unwittingly carburizing the iron and making steel. Hammering long enough (forging) to get the carbon content up to 1 percent produced a far stronger tool, one that could hold an edge better than one made of bronze. There is no written record of this process. Each batch of iron was different and a talented smith came to recognize which ores yielded the best results. The use of flux, an ingredient added to the iron-charcoal mix, reduced the temperature at which the slag melted, thereby making smelting easier.

>> Iron is one of the most common elements of the earth's crust but is seldom found in its natural state except in meteorites. Ancient Egyptians referred to iron as "black copper from the sky." When King Tutankhamen's tomb was discovered in 1922 it contained an iron dagger made from meteoric iron. The dagger was considered so precious that it did not travel with the rest of the tomb's contents.

THE INDUSTRIAL AGE AND BEYOND

Once iron and steel-making were understood, the focus shifted to making knives of greater weight, thus increasing their ability to cut with less effort. It became cheaper to produce knives and they became more readily available. Several cities in Europe became major centers for knife manufacturing: Sheffield, England; Thiers, France; and Solingen, Germany. In the United States there were knife manufacturers in Connecticut and Massachusetts, most founded in the early nineteenth century. All of these early manufacturing centers had three things in common: a nearby supply of iron ore, fast-flowing rivers or streams to run waterwheels, and an abundance of wood from which to make charcoal to fire the furnaces.

Prior to 1921, most kitchen knives were made from an alloy known as carbon steel, a combination of iron and carbon with few other trace elements. Many knife aficionados prefer carbon steel because it can take a keen edge. While the edge dulls rather quickly, it can be quickly steeled back into shape. Carbon steel's big drawback is that it will discolor almost immediately when it comes in contact with acidic foods and will discolor over time just from exposure to air. It will also rust if left damp, and letting a carbon steel knife go to rust will seriously impair its cutting edge. Carbon steel knives require diligent maintenance to keep them looking good and working well, and the average consumer usually doesn't want to bother with what is considered a high-maintenance knife.

During the 1920s, knife manufacturers began using stainless steel, which produced a blade that stayed sharper longer than the carbon steel blade. However, stainless steel is too hard to be sharpened on a steel. Its hardness is too close to that of a steel for the latter to have any effect.

The high-carbon stainless steel knives that most of us use today were developed after World War II and, in my opinion, prove to be the perfect compromise. If you look at the logo side of some high-carbon stainless knives, you will see the formula X 50 Cr MoV 15. The alloy used to make high-carbon stainless contains .5 percent carbon—the ingredient essential for turning iron into steel. The amount of chromium, molybdenum, and vanadium totals 15 percent, at least 13 percent of which must be chromium. This carefully balanced metallurgical cocktail prevents the oxidation that defaces the carbon steel knife and increases the strength and flexibility of the blade. All this science results in knives that are corrosion-resistant, that will maintain an edge for a reasonably long time, and that can be refreshed with a few strokes of the steel.

Above are two carbon steel chef's knives—one new, one old. The top one is a French-style knife made by Sabatier, one of the few manufacturers that still makes them. The bottom knife is made by Dexter-Russell. I purchased this knife in the late 1960s.

Note the discoloration despite the fact that it was given periodic scrubbing with scouring powder and a moistened Champagne cork. It is still sharp but if you look carefully, you will notice the original curve of the blade has been destroyed (by a street grinder who did not sharpen the edge properly).

MODERN KNIFE MAKING

There are three methods of knife making used today: drop-forging, precision forging, and stamping.

In August 2006, I had the opportunity to take a trip to Solingen and Deizisau, Germany, to visit the Wüsthof, Henckels, and F. Dick factories, as well as that of Julius Kirschner and Sons, the last remaining drop-forge in Solingen. Drop-forging, an old style

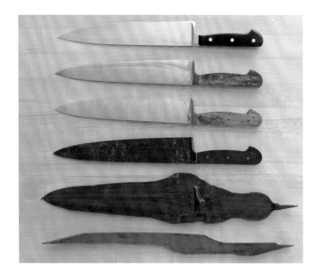

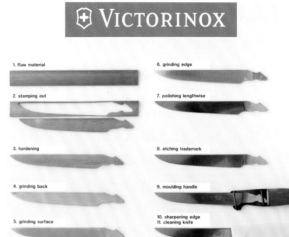

of knife making, is a loud, messy, sidewalk-cracking process that produces fine knives but is not especially friendly to the surrounding environment. I gained a great appreciation for how knives (and steels at F. Dick) were made.

The photo above, at left, shows various stages in the drop-forging process. From bottom to top they are: the cut blank, pressing after drop-forging, removing the flashing, the raw knife outline before tapering, the tapered and polished knife, and the finished product. The pieces in this photo were given to me by Wüsthof many years ago to show my students so that they could see firsthand the intricacies of knife making.

First a thick plank of alloyed steel is die-cut, heated, then placed in the drop-forge to produce a flat piece. The flashing is cut away and the knife blank is ready to begin the heat treatment process, during which the subsequent tempering (heating followed by quick cooling to harden the steel) and annealing (heating followed by slow cooling to prevent brittleness) temperatures are carefully controlled. The quick-cooling process known as quenching, usually in a vat of oil, is probably the most critical phase, in which the heated metal undergoes a quick and drastic drop in temperature.

The knife comes out of the heat treatment process looking pretty awful. It is still thick, so it must be taper-ground and then highly polished, which helps prevent corrosion. The handles are attached and polished, then the beveled edge is ground on. Finally the knife is given its last human and machine inspections.

Precision forging is quite different from the drop-forging method. The cut blank is heated in the center only to form the bolster and then is subjected to the same heat treatment, taper-grinding, polishing, handle attachment, and beveling processes as in drop-forging. Instead of die-cutting a blank from a thick steel plank, the blank is cut from rolls of steel.

The photo at right on page 16 illustrates the process used to make a stamped knife, in this case a boning knife. Not all knives have a full tang or bolster—those are just the top-of-the-line versions that knife manufacturers make. As you can see from the photo, after the flashing has been cut away (second from top left), this boning knife has neither, yet it is made by a company with a reputation for quality, even in their stamped line, and this is true for many manufacturers. The forged knife will usually have an advantage in overall quality but for some tasks, such as boning and filleting, a stamped knife will suffice.

Despite all the advances in both materials and processes, the basic structure of the knife has changed little. The forged knife still has a single-edge blade with a handle and some sort of bolster in between. The handle, originally of wood or sometimes horn, is now made of plastic or other composite material, but the basic design seems to have withstood the test of time.

2001

1987

1974

1965

1956
stainless

1956

1935

1886

CHAPTER TWO

The Anatomy of a Knife

Though a full tang chef's knife is depicted here, the same construction and terms apply to other knives as well. On a forged knife the blade, bolster, and tang are all one piece.

BLADE

The blade consists of the tip (the curved inch or two at the front), the edge (the part that does the cutting), and the heel (the widest part of the blade just in front of the bolster). The thick top of the blade is called the spine. Any mention of length—for example, 10-inch chef's knife—refers to the length of the blade, not the whole knife.

BOLSTER

The bolster is the thick piece of steel between the heel of the blade and the handle, and is what indicates that a knife is forged rather than stamped. The bolster provides weight and stability, protection for the fingers, and good balance. To test an 8- or 10-inch chef's knife for balance, place the bolster and heel across your index and middle finger. If the knife stays perfectly horizontal it is balanced. If the knife blade or handle is heavier it will want to tip. (Do this carefully and over a table or a cutting board, in case

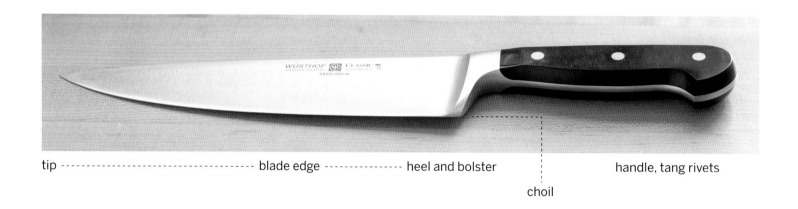

tip - blade edge - - - - - - - - - - - heel and bolster   handle, tang rivets

choil

The back view showing the spine   bolster   tang

A "full tang" handle

The bolster and finger guard.

An enclosed molded handle

the knife should fall.) You will have to compensate for a heavy blade by pushing down on the handle while you cut. It's a subtle feeling so you may not even be aware of it, but you will be using more energy than necessary. Likewise, a heavy handle will make you feel as though you are constantly forcing the blade to the board. In either instance, you are fighting your knife.

The flattened, curved portion of the bolster extending from the handle to the heel is called the finger guard. The part that extends from the spine to the heel and is ground to a point is the choil.

TANG

The tang is the section that extends from the bolster and to which the handle is attached by metal rivets. The handle and rivets should be flush with the tang to ensure a smooth grip and a sanitary surface with no spaces to harbor food particles. The end of the handle is called the pommel. Some pommels are straight, some are curved, and some look like a bird's beak and are called bird's beak pommels. The very back of the handle is referred to as the butt and can be used to mash garlic or herbs in a pinch if a mortar and pestle is not handy.

Don't get stuck on having a full tang knife. Many of the major companies make knives with a full tang as well as ones with plastic handles molded around a hidden tang. Even if you have a particular manufacturer in mind, check out both types. You might prefer the feel of the molded handle. Whatever style you choose, be sure to check the blade for balance before making a final decision.

PART II

THE KNIFE
KIT

CHAPTER THREE

Your Knife Wardrobe

In a video he made several years ago, the television food-and-travel personality Burt Wolf described a collection of knives as a wardrobe. I have never been able to verify when or with whom this term originated, but I like the concept. What should be in your knife wardrobe and what is actually lurking in your drawer or knife block are often two separate matters.

Not one to be reticent, the irascible Anthony Bourdain wrote in his book *Kitchen Confidential*, "I wish sometimes I could go through the kitchens of amateur cooks everywhere just throwing knives out from their drawers—all those medium-size utility knives, those useless serrated things you see advertised on TV, all that hard-to-sharpen stainless steel garbage, those ineptly designed slicers—not one of the damn things could cut a tomato."

While Bourdain was being a bit harsh—medium-size utility knives do have a purpose if they are quality tools and are used for the correct purpose—I have to concur with his general tone. Many of the things that go by the name "kitchen knife" are useful only as implements of self-torture, as they are poorly made, extremely dull, or both, forcing the user to work much too hard.

THE SELECTION PROCESS

In a December 2004 article in the *Los Angeles Times*, food columnist Russ Parsons wrote, "As far as I'm concerned, there are only two really important decisions in a cook's life: choosing a mate and buying a chef's knife. If that seems like an overstatement, you just haven't found the right knife." He doesn't elaborate about the mate but goes on to add, "The relationship between a cook and his knife is beyond mere utility. It is odd that cold steel could generate such emotion, but while a screwdriver is a tool, a good knife is a body part."

Whether cooking is as serious an endeavor to you as it is to Parsons, or just something you "have to do," it is important that you stock your wardrobe with good tools, the best you can afford. The selection process can be quite daunting because there are so many different types of knives on the market selling in such a wide price range that making a decision about what to purchase can become as confusing as buying a mattress. What follows will hopefully help you make the right choices.

The process starts by becoming a well-educated consumer. What you ultimately end up purchasing will depend primarily on what you prepare at home. If your lifestyle demands that you eat out every day and just prepare snacks and sandwiches, you will need fewer knives than if you are a serious daily, or even weekend, amateur cook. In the first instance, you can get by with two or maybe three knives. The serious cook usually needs no more than six knives.

The next factor in your decision is cost. Quality forged knives, which I highly recommend, cost considerably more than the $6.95 thing hanging on the rack at your local housewares store. Please leave it hanging there. It is a stamped, light, stainless steel knife that will be very difficult to keep sharp. A forged knife has some heft to it so it does the work for you and it is easy to keep its edge sharp. Such a knife is going to take some change out of your pocket, but doing the math will show it's a worthwhile cost.

A forged 10-inch chef's knife can cost about $120. If you maintain it properly, you will have it for twenty years or longer. Many of my knives are over twenty-eight years old because I do the necessary maintenance.

Suppose you use your knife four times a week.

20 years x 50 weeks (two weeks vacation) **= 1000 weeks**

1000 weeks x 4 uses per week = 4000 uses

$$120 \div 4000 \text{ uses} = 3¢ \text{ per use}$$

Getting your knife sharpened annually will cost $5.

$$5 \times 20 \text{ years} = 100$$

$$100 \div 4000 \text{ uses} = 2.5 ¢ \text{ per use}$$

So far that comes to 5.5 cents per use. If you want to sharpen your knives yourself, the cost of a honing steel might add another $\frac{1}{2}$ cent per use, bringing the total cost per use to 6 cents. If you use your chef's knife every day, the cost per use is even less.

Compare the cost of a good chef's knife to the cost of eating out or buying prepared foods because you are afraid of or don't know how to use knives or keep them sharp, a problem this book is going to solve, and that $120 knife is worth every penny.

Another consideration is the size of your hand, especially the length of your fingers. I observe the hands of my students very carefully and note those who have exceptionally long fingers. Their grip will feel cramped with a standard chef's knife whose widest point on the blade is between $1\frac{3}{4}$ and $1\frac{5}{8}$ inches. For them, I recommend a wider, heavier blade. Only a few companies make such a blade, so this might mean that you stock your wardrobe with knives from different manufacturers. This should not bother you; the desire to have matching knives should be trumped by the need to have the best,

most comfortable, most affordable tool you can in each of the categories I highlight in this chapter.

The handle, especially on your chef's knife, must feel comfortable; your grip should feel almost natural. There is a trend these days toward an ergonomic handle. The only way to assess a knife's ergonomics is to get it in your hand, preferably after you learn how to use it.

Notice that I have not mentioned appearance. The way a knife looks should not be your first consideration. No knife is ugly but some look better than others and are purchased solely on the basis of their visual appeal. Looks, however, can be deceiving. I have tested many a designer knife and found them wanting in many of the features I deem necessary. I'm always tempted to ask, "How many hours has the designer spent preparing food with that knife? Does he know how to use a knife properly? Does she understand that function should dictate form? Was the knife designed to be an effective cutting tool or a kitchen decoration?"

ASSESSING YOUR NEEDS

Assess your current wardrobe and buy only what you need, not want. I believe the average household can survive with between four and six knives. The chef's, utility, paring, and scalloped-edge (serrated) knives are typically the most useful. These are not necessarily listed in order of importance; that is determined by the user. In my kitchen, for example, the scalloped-edge knife is used far more frequently than the paring knife. However, the chef's knife, often referred to as the workhorse of the kitchen, is essential. If you get only one knife, get a chef's knife, preferably with a 10-inch blade. In addition to the four knives mentioned above, I would add a carving knife, then a boning knife—unless you are a vegetarian, in which case you need neither. If you do a lot of baking or are a dessert maven, you might want to add an offset knife, one whose blade drops below the handle.

BLOCK SETS

I generally don't recommend the purchase of block sets for several reasons:

1. No set that I know of comes with a 10-inch chef's, scalloped-edge, or carving knife, which I consider essential in any kitchen. The longest knife in any set I've seen is 8 inches.

2. The honing steel that comes with the set is usually too short (10 inches or shorter).

3. There are usually several knives bundled with the set that you might never use.

For these reasons, I suggest you buy your knives individually and pick up a separate knife block if that is how you want to store them. (See Safety and Storage, page 58.)

BUILDING A WARDROBE

Let's take a look at the knives I recommend you consider when building your wardrobe. Note the many options available in terms of blade length, handle style, and even handle color. The brands I use to illustrate the different types of knives come from the following manufacturers, all of whom have a long history of knife craftsmanship.

BRAND	MANUFACTURED IN	MANUFACTURED SINCE
Zwilling J.A. Henckels	Solingen, Germany	1737
F. Dick	Deisizau, Germany	1778
Messermeister	Solingen, Germany	1800
Wüsthof-Trident	Solingen, Germany	1814
Dexter-Russell	Southbridge, Massachusetts	1884
Sabatier	Thiers, France	1834
Lamson & Goodnow (LamsonSharp)	Shelburne Falls, Massachusetts	1837
Swiss Army (Victorinox and Forschner)	Forged in Solingen, Germany and finished in Ibach, Switzerland	1884
Kershaw	Portland, Oregon and Japan	1917
Thiers-Issard	Thiers, France	1958

Chef's Knife

FEATURES: Blade length: 5 to 14 inches. Heel width: 1¾ to 1⅝ inches for standard; 2¼ inches or more for wide blades.

USES: Preparing standard vegetable cuts (slices, strips, dices, and minces), chopping herbs, tapping off garlic skins, even skinning a fish fillet.

When you are choosing a chef's knife, weight and length count. The smaller the blade, the more force and stress *you* will have to apply, and the more strokes you will need to accomplish a given task. Ideally you want to work with the heaviest chef's knife you feel comfortable with. I recommend a minimum of 8 inches; 10 inches is ideal.

This will make more sense when you read the chapters on technique and understand how the knife functions.

What immediately distinguishes the chef's knife from all other knives is not its length but its weight and its width at the heel. When the cutting edge is placed flush to the board, and the handle held properly, there will be clearance between your knuckles and the cutting board. This is often referred to as the belly. The clearance permits the knife to glide smoothly across the cutting board for effortless cutting. The camber, or overall curve of the blade, will vary from manufacturer to manufacturer, and it should play an important part in your purchasing decision. Some people prefer a curved blade, some a straighter one.

On this page are five 10-inch knives (from top to bottom: Wüsthof, Henckels, F. Dick, Victorinox, and Sabatier). Note the differences in handle shape and type, bolster style, and blade curvature. The bottom two knives stand out the most. The Victorinox has had the bolster's choil removed to make the blade easier to sharpen. The Sabatier below it is an example of a French-style knife—the blade is somewhat straighter than the German-style knife and the bolster is replaced by a collarlike ring. French knives tend to be lighter (by about an ounce) and shorter (just shy of 10 inches) than their German counterparts, and I find this to be a disadvantage. I also like more curve to a blade.

At right are four 10-inch chef's knives with wide blades for those who have long fingers and need a bigger belly for more clearance. (From top to bottom: Wüsthof, Dexter-Russell, Messermeister, and a wooden-handled Dexter-Russell stamped knife.) Note the absence of the choil on the Messermeister and the absence of the bolster on the stamped knife. In addition, Messermeister polishes the spine, which helps prevent callous formation on the middle joint of the index finger. I wish all knife companies would do this.

Utility Knives

FEATURES: Blade length: 4½ to 7 inches, but I find the smaller ones almost useless. Heel width: Varies according to manufacturer. Some are as narrow as a paring knife.

USES: Slicing, dicing, and mincing large shallots, small onions, mushrooms, and medium-size fruits, and butterflying shrimp.

Utility knives are for those in-between jobs too small for a chef's knife but too big for a paring knife. The 5-, 6-, and 7-inch chef's knives and the Santoku should be considered utility knives.

Note the differences in style of the knives shown on page 29, especially the blade width, the shape of the handle, and the material from which it is made. The handle that stands out is the Henckels Twin Four Star II (third from the top). Also unique is the Shun Japanese-style bolsterless blade made by Kershaw, third from the bottom. Its Pakkawood handle is made from resin-impregnated hardwood veneers.

Paring Knife

FEATURES: Blade length: 3 to 4 inches, the most common and useful size being 3½ inches.

USES: Paring (trimming), peeling, coring, mincing, and slicing smaller fruits and vegetables, especially in the hand as Grandma used to do.

Its shape in both the German and French styles is very similar to that of the chef's knife but is obviously smaller and lighter with a narrower blade. A quality paring knife will often have the same features as its chef's-knife counterpart (bolster, full tang, and so on), though this is not essential. A three-quarter or even half tang will often suffice. A paring knife might lack a bolster but it must have a high-quality blade that can be readily honed and sharpened. It should not be too light—you still want to feel as though you have a knife in your hand. The paring knife cannot be put to the same balance test as the chef's knife, but do be wary of weighty and bulky handles that will make coring difficult.

These knives at left illustrate the different styles of paring knives. The last two on the right are French-style knives by Sabatier and Thiers-Issard. Their blades are considerably straighter than their German-style counterparts. The interesting Shun knife at the far left was designed for the Kershaw company by custom knife-maker Ken Onion for

Alton Brown, who wanted an angled paring knife that could cut things at the front edge of the cutting board without scraping his knuckles. This style of knife takes getting used to. Next to Onion's knife is another Shun product, a straight-bladed, bolsterless knife good for most tasks except coring, because the sharp point at the heel makes it difficult to support the knife without running into the point. Next to the Shun are paring knives by Messermeister, Henckels, F. Dick, Wüsthof, and LamsonSharp with its wood handle.

SLICING AND CARVING KNIVES

I differentiate between these two techniques and use different knives as for each. I slice when a roast is boneless and carve when it is on the bone. I will often use a scalloped-edge knife for slicing a crusty boneless roast as well as for other tasks.

Carving Knives

FEATURES: Blade length: 8 to 12 inches, the most useful size being 10 inches. A sharp tip is necessary for severing joints and working along the ribs and bones. Heel width: Varies according to manufacturer, but far narrower than the chef's knife with no belly, usually from $1\frac{1}{4}$ to $1\frac{3}{8}$ inches.

USES: Carving meat on the bone.

Scalloped-Edge Knife

FEATURES: Blade length: 5 to 18 inches. The longest of these is really for commercial use. I highly recommend a 10-inch blade. The tip of this blade is usually rounded or angled, but can also be pointed. Heel width: Varies according to blade length and manufacturer.

USES: Slicing items with crusts and skins, such as bread, bagels, sandwiches, tomatoes, eggplants, citrus fruits, melons, pineapples, boneless roasts, meat loaf, brownies, loaf cakes, strudel, puff pastry, and semisoft cheeses.

What is usually referred to as a serrated or bread knife is actually a scalloped-edge knife. The correct name is derived from the sharp teeth that run from tip to heel with scalloplike cutouts in between each tooth. Your steak knives are probably serrated. Compare them to a scalloped-edge knife and note the difference. To call this very useful tool a bread knife may have you thinking of it in very limited terms. The continuous movement of sharp teeth across a surface makes this knife effective on crusts and skins of all kinds. And because it is narrower and lighter than the chef's knife, it is less likely to crush delicate pastries.

As with the chef's knife, length counts. I do much of the above with a 10-inch blade, using few strokes. For very thin slices of lemon or cucumber, I will sometimes use a 5- or 6-inch blade.

Pictured above are three representatives of the smaller scalloped-edge family, (from top to bottom: Wüsthof, Messermeister, and Henckels' pointed-tip entry into the field). The Messermeister is called a tomato knife, but please use it on plum tomatoes only—it is too small for larger tomatoes. The Henckels is an example of a scalloped-edge knife with a pointed tip.

Scalloped-edge knives can be neither honed nor sharpened. The only way to renew this knife is to buy a new one. You can check the flat side of the blade for burrs and remove them by stroking it lightly on the steel, but the scalloped-edge side is off-limits. The scalloped-edge knife is the only knife for which there are left-handed and right-handed versions. Wüsthof makes a left-handed knife in a range of sizes and styles, as does Mundial, but you can also check on-line for other manufacturers.

GRANTON-EDGE SLICERS AND CARVERS

A Granton-edge knife is a knife that has hollowed-out grooves ground alternately on each side of the blade. It was originally developed in 1928 by the Granton company of Sheffield, England, to reduce the friction from fat and juices during the slicing of a juicy roast. The grooves create air pockets between the knife's surface and the roast and reduce suction to prevent sticking. The grooves are now appearing with some frequency on knives that don't need them, such as the chef's knife, paring knife, and Santoku. A Granton edge is useful on a carving knife but not nearly as effective as marketing would claim at preventing potato, celery, or anything moist from sticking to the blade. Also, in order for the grooves to be effective, they must come to the very edge of the blade, so if this knife is going into your wardrobe, be sure it meets your tough standards.

Pictured at right is a sampling of the knives mentioned above. The knife at the bottom is the Granton company's slicer. Above that is a Wüsthof 8-inch Granton-edge carver, an F. Dick scalloped-edge, sharp-tipped slicer/carver, a Wüsthof 10-inch scalloped-edge slicer, a LamsonSharp 10-inch scalloped-edge slicer with a pronounced curve to the blade and a wooden handle, a Henckels straight-edge carver, and Wüsthof's Super Slicer, whose scalloped edge is rounded. Bakers like the Super Slicer knife for cutting sheet cakes. It is also available in a left-handed version.

These are the basic knives I recommend for accomplishing most of your daily tasks. Should you start to expand your skills, consider adding the following to your wardrobe:

Pictured at left are Wüsthof, a wooden-handled Dexter-Russell, two knives by F. Dick with ergonomically designed, dishwasher-safe handles, Victorinox, and Henckels. Some of the knives shown have the classic curved heel, which is useful but not absolutely essential for getting into curved areas such as under a chicken wing.

Boning Knives

FEATURES: Blade length: 5 to 6 inches. Blade flexibility ranges from rigid to semiflexible. Some blades have a curved heel. Heel width: ¾ to ⅞ inch.

USES: Separating raw meat from bone and cutting through joints (but not hard bones).

A 5-inch rigid knife is ideal for fabricating (cutting up) chickens, or preparing and Frenching a rack of lamb or crown roast of pork. A 6-inch semiflexible blade can be used to fillet small fish.

Filleting Knife

FEATURES: Blade length: 6 to 8 inches. Blades have to be thin and flexible yet strong (some can bend at nearly a right angle). Heel width: ¾ to ⅞ inch.

USES: Filleting and carving fish meat, butterflying chicken breast.

Blade flexibility is important because the knife must be able to cut along the fish's bone structure. A filleting knife does not have to be fully forged, but it must have and hold a good edge and must be easily steeled. You want this critter sharp at all times. The blade should be long enough to remove the skin as well as fillet and cut the fish into portion-size pieces. Why use two or more knives if it can be done with one? If your filleting knife is not extremely flexible, it may double as a carving knife for small roasts.

Pictured at right, from top to bottom, Victorinox, Henckels, Knife Pro (a hollow-ground sample), Messermeister, Wüsthof, and Forschner.

The Knife Pro is our first look at a hollow-ground knife whose blade has two tapers. The polished portion starts at the spine and comes to within an inch or so of the edge, where a second unpolished taper begins and continues to the edge. Actually, the whole blade is polished from spine to edge, then the second taper is ground.

Hollow-ground knives are stamped from thin sheet steel, cheap to produce, and difficult to keep sharp as they are often made of hard stainless steel. Unless you have stretched your wardrobe's budget to the max and still need or want a filleting knife, I'd suggest avoiding the hollow-ground knives altogether.

SPECIALTY KNIVES

The following are what I'd call specialty knives. They belong in the "you may never need these but they might be nice to have" category.

Santoku

FEATURES: A lightweight, bolsterless, thin blade whose spine curves steeply to the point.

USES: It should be used to cut small items only. It is not useful for most chef's knife applications.

Let's get the confession out of the way—I rarely use mine! The good folks at Korin, a premier source for Japanese knives, told me that it actually originated in Japan and was made for Japanese women who wanted to cook Western-style food. One of the major housewares stores in America brought it to our shores. The rest is history.

No doubt the Santoku was then popularized by Food Network chefs and was often touted as an all-purpose knife. Bosh! There is no such thing as an all-purpose knife. Why would knife manufacturers bother making so many different knives if one knife could do it all? I find the Santoku to be too short and too light to use as a chef's knife (even if it were heavier it would still be too short), and too wide to use as a paring or utility knife. I could probably fabricate a chicken with it if I had to, but it wouldn't do well as a filleting knife. If you want one in your wardrobe, and in case you have never heard of a Santoku, here are three. (From top to bottom: Victorinox with no Granton edge, LamsonSharp, and Henckels.) By dint of its handle, the Henckels has more weight, but the weight is all in the handle and the blade is still too short for my liking.

Offset Knife

FEATURES: Blade length varies according to manufacturer, from 7 to 9½ inches. Heel width: 1 inch.

USES: Slicing quiches, pies, tarts, thick sandwiches, and baguettes.

One look at this knife, on page 37 at left, will tell you how it got its name. A scalloped-edge blade is set below the handle, making this the ultimate big-bellied knife with plenty of clearance for your

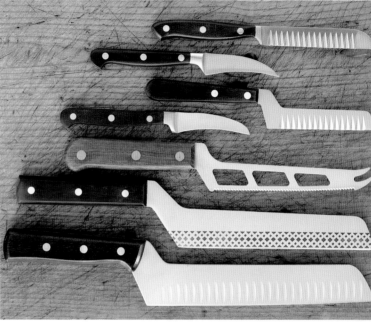

fingers when you want to section things like pies or quiche, or cut bread.

Pictured above at left, from top to bottom, are several examples of offset knives from: Messermeister, Wüsthof, Henckels, Dexter-Russell, F. Dick, and LamsonSharp.

Cheese Knives

FEATURES: The blades are usually offset and have an etched or fluted side to prevent sticking.

Pictured above at right are, from the bottom, three styles of cheese knives, by Forschner, Wüsthof, and LamsonSharp. The Wüsthof and Forschner

knives are best suited for hard cheeses; the LamsonSharp, for softer cheeses. I have lived many, many years without having a cheese knife, using a utility knife for the soft varieties and a scalloped-edge knife for harder cheeses.

Above the cheese knives are two tourne (or bird's beak) knives and two crinkle cutters for preparing crinkle-cut vegetables. The former are by Calphalon and Messermeister; the crinkle cutters are by Wüsthof and F. Dick.

A tourne knife is used to prepare those small, football-shaped, seven-sided potatoes, carrots, or turnips that come with your rack of lamb.

JAPANESE KNIVES

Since the 1980s, when the sleek, high-tech, Western-style Global knives were first imported, the American public has become enamored of Japanese knives. Korin, a store in lower Manhattan, opened its doors in 1982 and New Yorkers got their first look at hand-crafted Japanese knives made for professional chefs, as well as Western-style knives made for the home kitchen. Korin was kind enough to supply the knives at left.

It is important to make a distinction between traditional and Western-style Japanese knives. The latter look somewhat similar to the other knives in this chapter, but the similarities end there.

The traditional Japanese knife is a direct descendent of the *katana*, a sword that was called the soul of the samurai. The *katana* had to have two seemingly opposite attributes. It had to be flexible so as not to break on impact yet hard enough to retain its sharp edge in the heat of battle. The problem was solved by using two distinct types of steel. The core, made of a soft, low-carbon steel, was enclosed in a high-carbon jacket. The two were welded together during the forging process, giving the samurai a weapon that was both flexible and enduringly sharp.

The traditional Japanese knife, unlike the Western-style knife, is beveled on one side only, like a chisel. The other side of the blade is concave, which allows slices to fall away from the blade. Some chefs believe that the single-beveled blade makes cleaner cuts, but for those used to European knives, learning to use a traditional Japanese knife takes time and skill.

The Western-style Japanese knife is beveled on both sides but often not equally, in the manner of the European blade. The larger bevel is usually on the right side, so a left-handed person will need to special order a left-handed knife. Western-style Japanese knives are manufactured using mechanized, automated techniques similar to those found in Germany, but Japanese knives have a sharper, longer-lasting edge that is harder by several degrees on the Rockwell Scale and cannot be honed using a steel—they have to be sharpened on a stone, or better yet, professionally sharpened. They are definitely high-maintenance tools.

MAKING YOUR PURCHASING DECISIONS

You now have enough knife knowledge to make educated buying decisions. Go to a specialty cookware store that offers a selection of different brands and styles. If the knives are all shrink-wrapped, go somewhere else. Look for the features discussed in this chapter. Spend most of your time and money on the chef's knife since this is the most important knife in your wardrobe, one with which you will have a long-term, everyday relationship. Heft the knife—there will be slight differences between brands but the knife should have a weighty feel for its size and should feel balanced.

All the major manufacturers make several lines of knives aimed at a variety of markets. In terms of price, I believe that you get what you pay for.

All of the knife companies mentioned in this chapter and many others make perfectly reputable products and have their devotees. Ultimately you should buy what feels comfortable to you and what you can afford based on the knowledge you now have.

In the interest of candor and disclosure, Wüsthof knives have graced my knife block since before I even began using them in my Knife Skills classes in 1988. I wish I could remember who put me on to them. I have found their forged products to be consistently high in quality and, of utmost importance to me, easily maintained. I have gone as long as 13 months, using them three or four times a week at the various schools where I teach, without having to have them sharpened. Do I use any other brands of knives at home? Of course I do, and I have also tried many others that, for one reason or another, just have not passed muster.

CHAPTER FOUR

Knife Maintenance

No matter how much you paid for your knives, they will eventually lose their edge. It is up to you to keep that edge in good working condition and that means honing them regularly and getting them sharpened as needed.

There is a vast difference between sharpening and honing. Sharpening grinds a new edge on your knife; honing realigns this edge after it has dulled from use and puts it back into, or very close to, the original, just-sharpened condition.

THE KNIFE'S EDGE

The bevel, or angled edge, of any knife is set by the manufacturer, usually in the range of 15 to 20 degrees on each side, meeting at 0 degrees—sharp! Under a microscope, as in the picture at left from Chef's Choice, the edge will look like a row of sharp points, often referred to as "teeth," running the length of the blade. With normal use, the teeth start to bend and if you don't intervene by honing the blade the teeth keep bending until your cutting edge becomes rounded. Anything you try to cut will require more force. The knife can even slip on a slick surface such as a bell pepper and cut you instead. With regular home use, a knife needs to be sharpened only once a year, but should be honed before nearly every use. The frequency and duration of your prep sessions and the board on which you cut (see Cutting Boards, page 64) will affect how often you'll need to hone your blades.

After your knives, the most important part of your wardrobe is the steel. Knife manufacturers often and incorrectly refer to this tool as a sharpening steel. The confusion between sharpening and honing is prevalent enough without having the experts creating even more confusion. The process of maintaining that edge is referred to as steeling, honing, or truing, not sharpening.

So what exactly is a steel? It is a rod, pointed or rounded at the tip, with a handle. In between rod and handle sits the guard, and at the other end of the handle, a ring for hanging—long steels don't always fit in knife blocks. To get a bit more technical, a steel is a grooved, magnetized, hardened steel rod with a thin chromium plating to protect against corrosion. If you don't keep your steel dry, it will rust. A thicker plating would create more corrosion protection but would make the grooving of the steel more difficult.

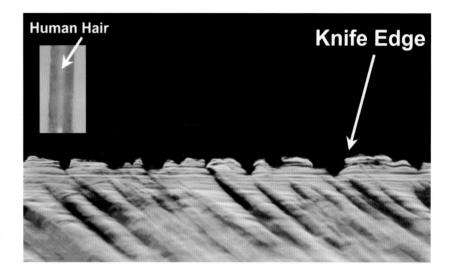

The steel has a Rockwell hardness of 64 to 66, harder than most Western manufacturers' knives, many of which are in the 55 to 58 range. It is this hardness differential that enables the steel to do its job.

CHOOSING A STEEL

Honing steels have been used by professionals for over one hundred thirty years. The leading steelmakers are the German firms F. Dick and Flügel, and the Sheffield, England firm of Egginton, all of whom make steels for various knife manufacturers in a wide range of styles. The length of the steel is your first consideration. Most range from 8 to 14 inches. Ideally it should be at least 2 inches longer that your longest knife. I have a 14-inch steel for my 12-inch chef's and carving knives.

Steels also come in a variety of shapes—four-sided, round, or varying widths of oval. The round or oval are further categorized as coarse, medium, or fine, depending on the closeness of the grooves running the length of the shaft. If you can find a cookware store that carries a selection of steels, run your thumbnail across each type and you'll feel the difference. On a quality steel, the grooves will end about ¾ inch before the guard. Some steels are polished so they have no grooves at all and are used primarily by meatpackers and retail butchers. I prefer an oval steel because it allows for more contact with the blade. When using it, make sure the knife's edge is placed against the broader side of the oval, not the narrow edge.

>> Beware! There are two devices on the market that resemble the honing steel. One is coated with fine diamonds, the other is made from a white industrial ceramic, Neither of these align the knife's edge but function more as a sharpening device. Don't let an inexperienced salesperson sell you one as a honing steel. If it is labeled or touted as a diamond, it is a sharpening and not a honing tool.

You can easily make do with one medium steel, though I am a strong proponent of a two-steel method—medium and fine cut. The latter acts like a stropping device. If you're old enough to remember the razor-wielding barber, you'll recall the strop, that long piece of leather hanging from the side of the chair. After or even during use, the barber slapped the razor against the strop away from the edge on both sides to remove any small burrs or nicks. Though you can get a very workable edge without it, what the medium steel doesn't smooth out, the fine one will. It depends on how serious you want to get about your knife's edge. I will often try the fine steel first and, if satisfied with the results, proceed to do my work. If not, I'll use the medium steel, then follow up with a few swipes of the fine steel. F. Dick makes a wide, flat steel called the "multi-cut" with deeper grooves that they claim will sharpen a blade by using hard pressure and finer, shallow grooves that will hone with lighter pressure. You can easily identify it, third from the right, in the photo on page 43. My favorite Italian butcher in Brooklyn uses it exclusively on his rented boning knives but still sends them out to be reground every week.

The handle of a steel can be made of wood, polyethylene plastic, stag horn, or even stainless steel and comes in a variety of grips. I get the best nonslip grip from a wooden, beehive-shaped handle, second and fourth from the left on page 43. You may prefer another style and handle material, so be sure to try several different kinds. I also like a ring at the end of the handle for hanging the steel in a convenient spot on a nearby nail or hook—especially handy for a longer steel that won't fit in a standard knife block.

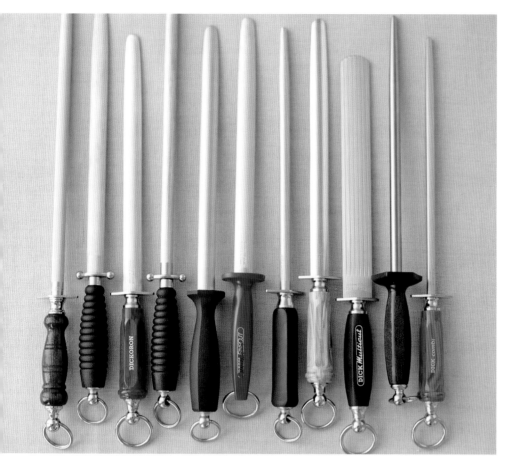

The guard that sits between the shaft and the handle not only prevents the steel from rolling off the counter; it also protects against self-mutilation should you choose to hone by holding the steel parallel to your torso and pulling or flicking the knife from the tip of the steel to the guard. Experienced butchers and chefs do this up to 200 times a day and still get cut.

Most of my students find it difficult and scary, and, frankly, it is more difficult for a beginner to maintain the angle on the steel using this method. For the method of steeling I generally use, I prefer a narrow guard, either diamond shaped or beaded at both ends. A wide guard, second from the right, gets in the way of placing the knife at the handle end of the steel.

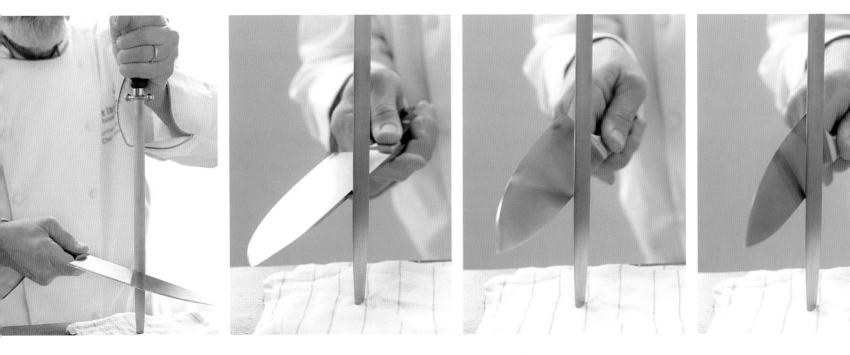

HOW TO HONE A KNIFE

You need to know the angle at which your knife was beveled by the manufacturer, usually 15, 17, or 20 degrees. The standard bevel for chef's knives is 20 degrees. Narrower and shorter knives may differ. Hopefully this information will be supplied in whatever literature comes with your knives. It might be printed on the paper sleeve. Try to replicate the original bevel in the honing process.

Place a towel on your counter or cutting board. Grasp the handle of the steel and place the tip on the towel. Two angles concern you—the bevel angle and the tip-handle angle. To practice the bevel angle, place the spine of the knife against the steel at a right angle (90 degrees). Cut that angle in half to 45 degrees. Cut that angle in half again to 22.5 degrees, then come in a smidgen more for a 20-degree angle. Eyeball what this position looks like and remember this picture. Try to be precise but don't get too obsessive. The honing police won't show up if you're at 18 degrees, and you won't do any damage to your edge.

Place the edge of your blade against the steel at the bevel angle. Place the heel of the knife near the top of the steel where the grooves end at a right angle from the tip of blade to the handle. (This is where a wide

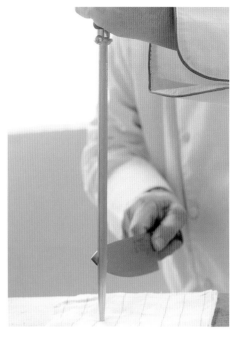

guard gets in the way—you'll have to move the knife farther down the steel.) Now angle the tip of the knife up to achieve a 45-degree angle. Using and maintaining moderate pressure, pull the knife back and down from heel to tip and from the top of the steel toward the bottom until the tip is pulled off the steel in a follow-through motion. Keep your eyes focused on the edge angle as you progress down the steel. Do not turn your wrist during this motion as it will change the angle.

Right-handers generally start on the right side of the steel, then move to the left. Pretend you are cutting a V notch into both sides of the steel. No fancy, curly calligraphy here. Generally, four or five strokes of moderate pressure will do just fine. Better yet, do three using moderate pressure and lighten the pressure for the last one or two strokes.

CARING FOR THE STEEL

A honing steel is magnetized. All the microscopic filings that come off the edge of the blade as you hone the knife are attracted to the steel. Wipe the steel from guard to tip with a soft cloth after each use. Every so often, wash the steel with hot soapy water, rinse it, and dry it thoroughly. Unlike your knives, which are most likely high-carbon stainless, the honing steel will rust if left damp. I am often

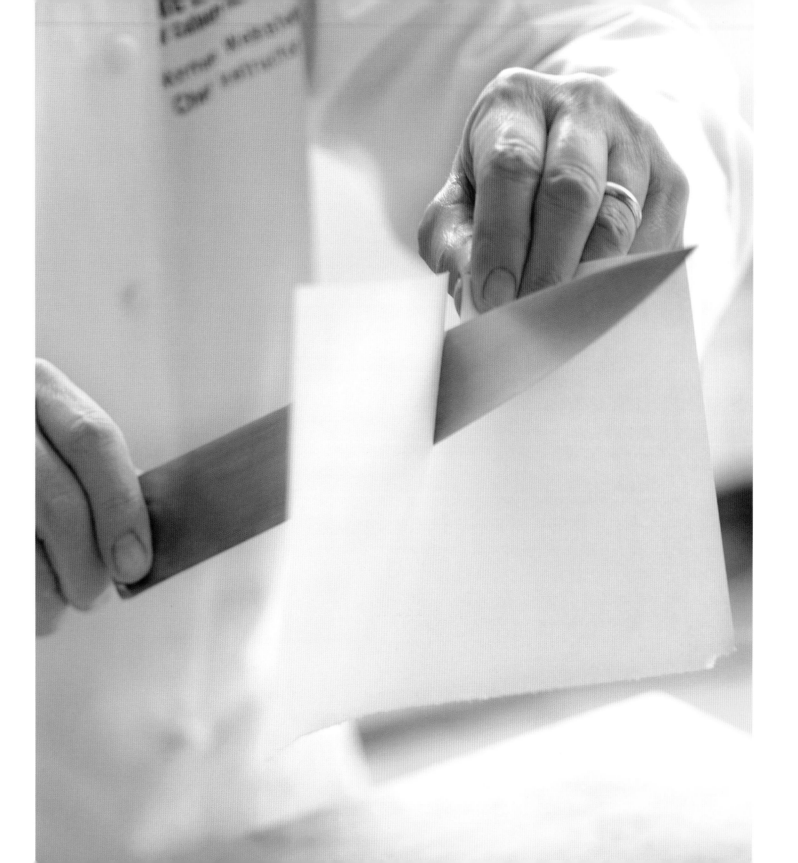

asked how long a steel will last. After several years of constant use the grooves of the steel will wear down. If you have mastered the ability to realign your knife's edge and suddenly notice that what used to work no longer does, run your thumbnail across the grooves. If you can no longer feel them, it's time to replace your steel. Generally, with normal use, a steel will last three to four years.

TESTING FOR SHARPNESS

There are several ways to test a knife's edge for sharpness, though no one method is met with universal agreement by the experts. I pull the first joint of my thumb across—I said across, not along—the blade at several different points. Depending on how you've used the knife, the edge might not be evenly sharp. If you've done a lot of cutting near the heel, that area might need a little more attention. There will be some bite or resistance as you do this. If you feel no bite whatsoever, the blade could use a few strokes on the steel. Sometimes the edge will feel excessively sharp, almost jagged. If that is the case, I will use the fine steel to smooth the edge. A newly purchased or sharpened knife should not feel jagged.

You can also check for sharpness by cutting a piece of 20-lb. bond paper. Hold the paper up in front of you and pull the knife from heel to tip at a downward angle. If the edges of the paper are cleanly cut and there is no resistance as you pull, your knife is sharp enough to do most jobs. If it catches somewhere along the way, that part of the knife may still be dull. This usually occurs near the tip. Try a few more strokes. If the blade really catches, you might still have a folded edge on one side of the blade. To fix this, put the tip of the steel on the towel on your counter or cutting board at a 45-degree angle. With the edge of the blade facing the tip of the steel, and with as close to the correct bevel angle as you can get, gently pull the blade from heel to tip along the steel, then check the edge again.

SHARPENING

You really have only two options for putting a new edge on your knife—do it yourself or give it to a professional. Even if you've been really faithful about using the honing steel, eventually that delicate edge is going to show signs of wear and become round and thick. What was easily cut before now needs more force, exactly what you don't want. I generally suggest that you locate a professional cutler in your area, one whose main business is sharpening kitchen knives and scissors, not axes and chisels—and get references. Sharpening is time-consuming and takes a good eye and a steady hand, as a bevel is measured in microns, not inches. Unfortunately, such talent is becoming increasingly difficult to find. New York City used to have over thirty cutlers; now there are no more than three. If your search for a reputable cutler has failed, you'll have to get a new edge on that knife yourself.

GRINDING SERVICES VERSUS CUTLERS

A grinding service deals primarily with the retail and wholesale butchering or fish-mongering trades, who work with fairly cheap, hollow-ground, stainless steel knives that are used for a week, then returned in exchange for some newly reground knives. The shelf life of these knives can sometimes be as little six to eight weeks, at which point they are discarded. Unless a grinding service can assure you that your prized possessions will be treated with loving care, be cautious. Don't assume that giving your knives to the local butcher will solve your sharpening problem.

As for the itinerant grinder, the green truck that appears in your neighborhood from time to time—I can't, in all fairness, speak for all of them, but in my ignorant, young, and foolish days, I have had more than one knife's edge destroyed by this species. They are generally equipped to deal with sturdier tools (axes and chisels) and not with the very delicate edge of a good chef's knife. Get references beforehand and ask to see a sample of his finished product.

Speaking of the finished product, let's compare two chef's knives at left. Note that on the top knife, the choil curves back from the heel. The bottom knife has been improperly sharpened. The choil is wider than the heel—not by much, but enough to make a gouge in your cutting board every time you push the knife forward. If you are using a service for the first time I suggest that you take a picture of the heel area of each knife you are sending to be sharpened so you can make an immediate comparison of what you sent and what you got back. Also, be aware that most cutlers will sharpen an edge at 20 degrees regardless of the manufacturer's bevel, unless you specify otherwise.

DO-IT-YOURSELF SHARPENING TOOLS

Honing is not easy. It takes practice. Sharpening is harder. It takes even more practice. There are dozens of devices being sold as sharpeners. Some work well and are fairly easy to use, some require a degree in mechanical engineering, and some should be thrown into the garbage. Sorting through them all is far beyond the scope of this book so we'll deal with the most readily available tools that are fairly easy to handle.

At right, clockwise from the top you will see oil and Japanese water stones, a diamond steel, a ceramic steel, three types of diamond sharpeners, and a handheld, pull-through sharpener.

Of the two steels shown, the diamond is more aggressive at removing steel from the knife's edge. The ceramic steel is more of a polishing tool. The diamond whetstone is available both as an inter-

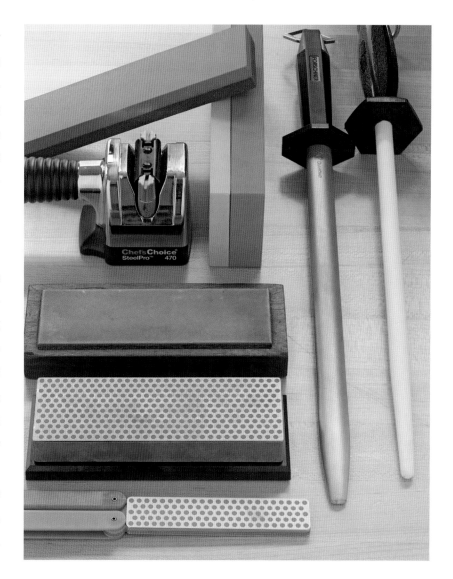

rupted (polka-dot) or a smooth, continuous surface Surface textures can be extra coarse, coarse, fine, or extra fine depending on the size of the diamonds embedded in the metal plate. The coarser the surface, the more steel particles will be removed from the edge of your knife. Coarse should be used only if your knife is extremely dull. The diamond whetstone is a fast remover of swarf (the material to be removed from the knife). If you prefer to use a diamond stone, opt for the fine texture and make sure the diamonds are of the monocrystalline type. Diamond stones are expensive but they will last longer than water stones and do not require flattening.

Keep in mind that any tool designated as "diamond" is hard: 100 on the Rockwell scale. Therefore, steels, stones, or pull-through devices containing diamonds should be considered sharpening and not honing tools. Use them every day and in six months your chef's knife will be a carving knife. There are many pull-through tools in the marketplace. If you do not know, or the dealer can't tell you, what you are pulling your knife through—diamonds, ceramic, carbide, or honing steel rods—don't buy it.

SHARPENING STONES

Most serious do-it-yourselfers opt for using a sharpening stone, often referred to as a whetstone or a bench stone. The choice usually comes down to water stones or oil stones, so named in reference to the lubricant used on the surface of each. Both are available in their naturally mined state, but the manufactured products do a perfectly acceptable job and are much more affordable. (A natural Japanese water stone can cost $2000.)

Whether natural or synthetic, oil, water, and diamond stones come in different grain sizes determined by the number of particles in the matrix. Oil and water stones have numbers assigned by the manufacturer. Water stones usually have the number clearly marked on the stone or box. The higher the number, the finer the grit. Oil and diamond stones are usually labeled as extra coarse, coarse, medium fine, fine, or extra fine. Think of the stone the same way you would the steel. A coarse-cut steel will align the edge but leave scratch marks. The scratches will get smoothed out as you progress to a medium-then a fine-cut steel, which will polish those scratch marks, leaving a smooth, sharp edge. Likewise, the coarser the stone, the more steel it will remove from your knife's edge and create deeper scratch marks. Use a coarse stone only if there are nicks in the blade (and there shouldn't be any nicks unless you have been chopping bones or doing something you were not supposed to).

Water stones range in grit size from 150 up to 8000. For the average home user who will not be sharpening every day or even every week, the most useful grit sizes are 1000 and either 3000 or 6000.

The 1000/3000 combination stone is usually sufficient for home use and will give the best results for your money.

Synthetic water stones are made by fusing the abrasive particles with a porous bonding agent. The latter breaks down with use, exposing a new layer of particles as you work. Pushing the knife across the stone will result in a slurry of steel particles. Do not wipe the slurry away until the sharpening process is completed; it actually assists in the process. Water stones tend to wear more quickly than oil or diamond stones and must be periodically planed with a stone fixer to keep the surface absolutely level. Remember, though, that you are only going to use this stone once or twice a year, so we're not talking high maintenance. The 1000 grit stones need to be submerged in water for 10 or 15 minutes or until the bubbles stop surfacing. After each use, the stone should be washed and allowed to dry completely before storing.

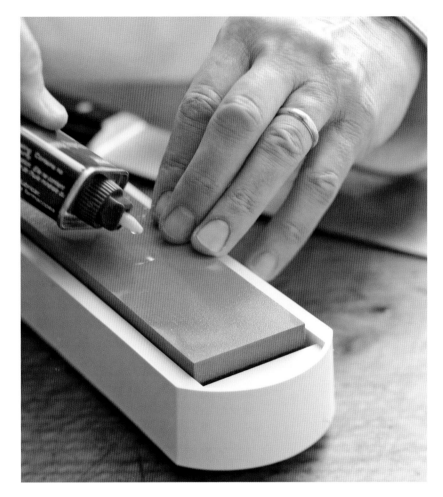

As with water stones, the synthetic oil stones will suffice for all but the purists. One of the major manufacturers of oil stones, Norton Pike, offers two synthetic stones, Crystolon and India, as well as natural Arkansas stones. Both the Crystolon and India versions are available in coarse, medium, and fine grits. Crystolon, a silicon carbide product, is gray or black; the aluminum oxide India stone is brown or orange. Crystolon stones tend to be more aggressive. If you hone on a regular basis, I'd recommend a medium and a fine India stone. You will have four sides to work with and they should last a lifetime. Neither the Crystolon nor the India fine stones will get you a highly polished edge—you'll need a natural soft Arkansas stone for that. Frankly, for most households, the fine India stone will give you a sufficiently sharp and smooth edge. The exception is if you do a lot of meat fabrication, in which case you might consider putting your boning and filleting knives through the cycle of medium and fine India followed by soft Arkansas.

Synthetic oil stones are filled with oil at the factory but the stone manufacturers still recommend glazing the surface with their oil before each use, as on page 51. Wash oil stones with soap and water, rinse, and allow to dry thoroughly before storing in a closed box, as dust and dirt can clog the surface.

You will want your stone to be large enough so you can achieve a smooth, fluid motion when using it. Most stones are 8 inches long and at least 2 inches wide. As for style, your options are a free-standing stone or a stone that fits in a base, which helps in anchoring the stone during use.

My 6000-grit Japanese water stone is fixed in its base. The free-standing water stone can be set on a wet towel; the oil stone cannot, so if you opt for no base (a base is usually included as part of a two- or three-stone system), just use a towel or rag to prevent it from moving about during use. The manufacturer suggests putting oil in the base, but I find this messy, and oil only the exposed surface I am using.

ELECTRIC SHARPENERS

The electric sharpener bears mentioning because of its nearly universal availability in cookware stores and on cookware Web sites. If this is the sharpening route you choose, I urge you to read the instructions carefully and more than once. The Chef's Choice Model 120 three-slot electric sharpener is on the opposite page. The slots are designed to sharpen, hone, and polish the edge. It sounds simple, but once you turn on the switch, you cannot control the speed at which the diamonds move along the edge of your knife. You must learn how to set and pull the knife through the slots. If the knife is kept in the start position at the heel for too long, you will eventually have a swailed knife, one whose choil is wider than the heel. Remember, you are working with diamonds and they can damage your knife if used improperly. You will not have as much control of the edge as you would with sharpening stones, where you control the bevel angle and the applied force.

Another thing to consider is that the diamond slots leave scratch marks on the edge of the knife. I am also concerned that the machine will alter the bevel of most knives if used in all three phases. I have used the polishing slot on the right side and noted that it did smooth out the edge of my knife.

Professional cutlers and serious do-it-yourselfers usually eschew the electric sharpener. The former use professional machines costing hundreds, even thousands of dollars, none of which utilizes diamonds. Instead, the knife's edge is placed on a series of belts or wheels of increasing fineness and are often finished on a cotton buffing wheel to polish the edge. The belt sits in a reservoir of water to keep the knife edge from getting too hot. Sharpening, even on a machine, is a serious skill and takes a long time to learn. Believe it or not, the knife-sharpening trade can be lucrative.

HOW TO SHARPEN A KNIFE

Think of the sharpening process as shaving off a very thin layer of steel to get at a fresh layer underneath. You are trying to push the knife's bevel from the shoulder, the point where the blade's polished taper begins, to the 0-degree edge. The steel is very thin at that point so not much force is required. As the steel is pushed in this direction a burr, or thin wire edge, forms on the opposite side, the side facing up. The burr should form along the entire edge and is a natural result of one bevel being pushed against another.

There are proponents of pulling the knife across the stone from heel to tip, pushing across the stone from tip to heel, and making circular or even figure-eight motions. I prefer to use the method taught to me by Chiharu Sugai of Korin Japanese Trading

Corporation of Manhattan, a purveyor of fine Japanese-made knives, because his technique uses a movement of the knife on the stone that is similar to the way I use my chef's knife. I periodically reinforce these techniques by viewing his DVD (see page 218). The process can be used with all sharpening stones.

If using a Japanese water stone, gather everything you need to get started. Soak the stone and stone fixer in water for about 10 minutes. When the soaking water no longer bubbles, the stone and stone fixer are ready to use. Use a fixer to achieve a 45-degree angle along the long and short sides of the stone. Three or four moderate strokes are sufficient—right-angle edges could scratch the knife. Run your hand over the top, checking to see if it is concave. If so, flatten it with the fixer.

Establishing the angle may be the most difficult part of the sharpening process. You are trying to place the knife's bevel on the stone. If the knife's spine is raised too high, only the bevel's front edge is in contact with the stone; too low and you are on the back edge and the shoulder of the blade.

Once the angle has been established, you are ready to sharpen the first side using the medium (1000 grit) stone. Since the bevel is the same on each side, it does not make a great difference which side you begin with, but I usually start with the logo side down.

Sprinkle some water on the surface of the stone. Place the thumb along the spine and the index finger on the heel. Place the blade at about a 40-degree angle (four o'clock) with the heel in the bottom right

corner of the stone. Raise the spine about ¼ inch and place your middle three fingers directly on the knife's edge. They should not touch the stone. It is of utmost importance that you understand that sharpening takes place under the fingers.

Using moderate and constant pressure, pull the knife straight up the center of the stone with the fingers, while pushing with the other hand taking care not to raise the spine.

Release the pressure and pull the knife back to the start position. Before you make the next stroke, move the knife ahead, under your fingers, about ½ to ¾ inch. Do not spread your fingers apart.

Pull and push the knife forward again to sharpen a new section along with some of the old. Repeat this process until you have reached the bolster. The whole process will probably take eight to ten strokes. Check the slurry marks; they should travel right up the center of the stone.

Depending on the starting condition of the edge, you might have to repeat the whole process three or four times until you have raised a burr on the top side of the edge. Check by running your thumbnail over the edge. Once you have a burr, you can sharpen the other side.

Turn the blade over and change finger positions. Place the thumb on the heel and the index finger on the spine and repeat the steps used for the first side using the same bevel angle.

If the knife has a pronounced bolster and it is get-

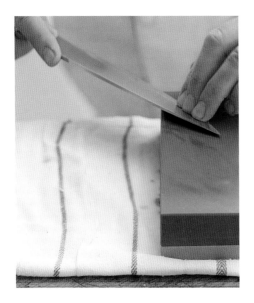  

ting in the way, gradually turn the knife horizontally as you get towards the middle of the blade. Sharpen until you feel a burr on the top side. Remove the burr by giving the just-sharpened side a few gentle strokes with a fine stone or even a ceramic steel if you have one, or by gently pulling the burred side diagonally across the stone.

After the initial sharpening process on the medium stone (1000 grit) you are ready to use the same process on the fine stone (3000 or 6000 grit). You are not trying to raise a burr, but instead to polish the edge by smoothing out any scratch marks made by the medium stone. Prepare the fine stone and place it in the same position on the towel as the medium, and keep the knife in the same starting position. If you are using

a combination water stone it has already gone through the soaking process but it is a good idea to dribble water on the surface again before putting the knife to it.

After the blade has gone through both the sharpening and polishing phase, there still may be microscopic particles on the edge. They can be removed by stropping the blade edge on several sheets of damp newspaper or by using very light strokes on a fine-cut or ceramic steel, or even on a genuine leather strop. Strop away from—not into—the edge.

The three components of the sharpening process, the pull-push, release, and repositioning of the knife, are not easy to master. Before I put knife to stone, I practiced the technique slowly on a cutting board to acquire the coordination of all the movements, doing one motion at a time, then adding the next and the next until I began to feel comfortable. I was not thrilled with my first attempt at the real thing but soon began to note improvement and success—sharp knives. Though I do not have the ease and speed of Master Sugai, I feel rather comfortable putting my fine Western knives on the stone. I'm still working on getting the hang of sharpening traditional and Western-style Japanese knives whose respectively single and uneven bevels present a new challenge.

If everything you've learned about sharpening seems overwhelming, don't worry. Look on page 218 for a list of cutlers, many of whom do mail-order business.

KNIFE REPAIR

Bad things happen to good knives. Knife tips generally do not bend or fall off, nor do chips or nicks suddenly appear in the blade for no reason. Accidents do happen—knives occasionally fall from hands or tables. But most bad things are the result of neglect or abuse—bones are chopped, knives clang against pans in the dishwasher, cans are pried open, hedges get trimmed.

An experienced cutler can straighten a tip or maybe a slight bend in the edge, but a knife has to be reground to reestablish the point or get rid of a serious nick. The integrity of the knife, its curve and balance can be seriously compromised. So, let the butcher hack the bones, don't put your knives in the dishwasher, buy a can opener and a hedge trimmer, and only use your knives for their intended purpose.

A FINAL THOUGHT

Hone (steel) and sharpen (stone) your knives regularly. Keeping your knives in good working condition is easier if the knife is still relatively sharp. Aligning the edge can be accomplished with moderate pressure and fewer strokes on the steel if the teeth have not been allowed to fold too much, in which case you will need more strokes and firmer pressure while honing. Similarly, waiting until the knife is very dull can increase the time on the stone by as much as 10 minutes until the burr forms. Think of honing and sharpening as the oil change and tune-up for your knives. By doing both regularly, you increase the life and well-being of your knife wardrobe.

CHAPTER FIVE

Safety and Storage

SAFETY FIRST

You already know that keeping your knives sharp is important not only for effective cutting, but also for safety reasons. A dull knife is a dangerous tool that forces you to work harder. This extra effort can result in a slip, which can result in a serious cut. There are lots of things you can do to minimize the number of knife-related injuries in the kitchen.

Not surprisingly, America's number one kitchen accident is the hand-cut bagel. Never use a knife to cut anything you are holding in the palm of your hand. Always slice on a cutting board. Never remove food from your knife with the blade edge facing your palm.

Keep all knife edges covered. Place knives in a block or, if storing them in a drawer, keep the edges protected by enclosing them in plastic sheaths so you don't nick your fingers as you hurriedly reach for your favorite. Sheaths come in a variety of sizes to protect all but the longest knives. For those longer or wider knives that won't fit into a block or store-bought sheath, make your own from a piece of corrugated board and strapping tape (see bottom knife at left).

Keep all knives out of the reach of children. I strongly recommend a locked drawer for knives. Children are curious. They find stuff.

Don't leave knives in a sink full of dishes, and don't place knives with tips pointed upward in the silverware compartment of your dish drainer or dishwasher rack. They don't belong in any of these places at any time. After each use, wash your knives by hand in hot soapy water using a cotton dishcloth. Dry them immediately and put them safely away. Never wash or dry a knife with the blade edge facing your palm.

When transporting knives in the kitchen, hold the handle firmly. Carry the knife parallel to your legs, tip pointed downward, blade facing back, until you reach your destination.

To hand someone a knife, hold it by the spine with your hand centered over the bolster, tip facing you, handle facing the recipient. Do not let go until the recipient says, "got it." Or place the knife on the cutting board or counter and let the next person pick it up.

Always keep your knife in view on the table or board. Don't cover it with a casually thrown towel or apron. You might forget where you left it and it could go flying when you go to wipe a spill or don your apron.

Don't carry a cutting board with a knife on it. The knife could slip off the board as you head towards the sink or counter. Make two trips; otherwise one

of them might be to the emergency room, where you can commiserate with the person who did the bagel thing.

Keep your cutting board stabilized at all times to prevent it from slipping on a smooth work surface such as polished wood, granite, tile, or Corian. Use a nonskid plastic or rubberized material (available in office supply stores) between your board and counter. A 6 x 6-inch piece centered under the board will prevent the board from slipping. Some people like to use a wet towel, but this is not good for wooden cutting boards.

Don't let a knife handle hang off the edge of your cutting board. If you are still prepping food and need to leave the prep area, keep the knife within the confines of the board. This one got me—during a class. It was a less painful lesson for the students than for me. I accidentally hit the handle and the blade came up and back. I could not get my hand out of the way fast enough so I paid the penalty for my lapse of attention. The good news is that the knife was sharp and the cut healed quickly.

Don't try to catch a falling knife. Step back and let it drop. Knives can be easily replaced—fingers and toes take more work.

And, finally, while you won't get arrested for cutting under the influence, it is generally not a good idea to mix alcohol and knives.

Thinking safety is the number one rule.

STORING YOUR KNIVES

Where you store your knives is as much a matter of safety as it is about the organization of your work environment.

Knife Blocks

There was a time when a knife block was only sold as part of a set, and that is still the most common way to acquire one. I have my quibbles with sets, as they never contain some of the longer knives I find useful—the 10-inch chef's, carving, or scalloped-edge knives. It is now possible to buy your block independent of your knives.

Knife blocks come in two basic shapes: upright or angled. I find the upright style to be impractical in most situations. From a mechanical point of view, it is more difficult to remove your knife from the block. You must pull the knife straight up. For those of average height this is more awkward than removing it from an angled block.

In addition, it is difficult to place the upright block on any counter with cabinets above it unless there is an extraordinary amount of space between counter and cabinet. This type of block works if

CHAPTER SIX

Cutting Boards

Joe Ng, one of New York's top dim sum chefs, and I were dining on his delicacies one day and talking about knives and boards, when he said, "The knife and the board are a family." I realized that by family, he meant a caring and respectful family. He reveres and respects the tools of his trade, as do all chefs, and understands the interrelatedness of the implements in his kitchen. After your honing steel, the cutting board is the most important member of the family.

Your knives and cutting board are going to be lifelong companions. If you choose the wrong board, you will have a dysfunctional family. It is difficult for the knife to damage the board, but easy for the wrong board to hurt the knife by quickly dulling its delicate edge.

THE HISTORY OF THE BUTCHER BLOCK

The modern cutting board evolved from the butcher block, whose origins go back to the last quarter of the nineteenth century. Two of the companies largely responsible for this innovation are still in business today: the Michigan Maple Block Company, founded in 1878 and John Boos & Company of Illinois, founded in 1887. According to the Maple Block website, the cutting block used by butchers at the time was a section of southern sycamore log. The board's size was limited by the log's girth, and it tended to split as it dried, which caused it to harbor bacteria, making the surface unsanitary. The company decided to swap sycamore for maple, which is native to and abundant in the area. Instead of using a section of log, they glued strips of wood together with the ends (from the exposed stump) facing up. The result was a far more durable product not limited in width or height.

John Boos & Company also made cross-section blocks from local sycamore. Blacksmiths were using these blocks to support their anvils and absorb the blows from their hammers. Commercial butchers noticed this practice and began ordering the blocks for their shops. In 1892, the company moved from a blacksmith's shop and began producing butcher blocks. Eventually, both companies realized that a broader market beckoned and began production of the modern cutting board.

MODERN CUTTING BOARDS

The two most common cutting boards found in today's homes are made either from wood or some type of plastic, a petroleum derivative. Before the advent of plastics, wood was the only surface on which food was cut. It seems as though every year, a new study comes out stating that wood is safer than plastic, or that plastic is safer than wood. Scientist Dean O. Cliver brought to our attention through several studies the fact that wood has natural antibacterial properties. There are ample studies produced by independent researchers and academics that support both sides of the wood-versus-plastic safety issue. One of the main concerns centers around the cuts the knife makes on the surface of the board and the ability of those cuts to harbor bacteria. Some studies have concluded that this is more of a problem with plastic since it cannot be resurfaced, while others have concluded that the same can be said of wooden boards (though I have done so with sandpaper). So the battle rages on without a knockout punch on either side.

There is also the issue of convenience. Commercial food institutions, cooking schools, and restaurants generally prefer plastic boards because they require

ferent boards for meats and vegetables. Plastic boards are available in different colors. J.K. Adams of Vermont makes a board with a chicken imprinted on one side and some vegetables imprinted on the other. No matter which solution you choose, you are still going to have to observe the basic rules of board safety and sanitation. Regardless of material, after each use, cutting boards have to be cleansed with soap and hot water, rinsed, and then dried.

WOODEN BOARDS

Though there are cutting boards made from the complete cross section of a tree's trunk, most are manufactured from air- and kiln-dried planks. The drying process can take weeks or months depending on the original moisture content of the wood. The end product will have a 6- to 8-percent moisture content. (This will become important when you read about board care later on.)

far less maintenance than wood. I was therefore pleasantly surprised to see wooden boards in the kitchen of the Culinary Institute of America in St. Helena, California, on a visit several years ago. After the class, the boards were taken to the sink, washed, and dried.

I have personally used nothing but wooden boards since I started cooking for myself in the early '60s. I have never had a foodborne illness in my house nor, to the best of my knowledge, has anyone ever become ill from food that I have prepared, and I have taught in cooking schools that used wooden boards, plastic boards, or thin plastic sheets (I hated those).

For those who are still not convinced that the simple steps to food safety are sufficient, use dif-

The wood is then cut to the specifications, glued with a non-toxic glue, clamped, machine sanded, shaped (rounded corners, beveled edges, routed handles, or all of the above), then oil finished, usually by dipping the board in the mineral oil solution, lifting it, and letting it air-dry.

Cutting boards are assembled in one of three ways—exposing end grain, edge grain, or flat grain.

You can quickly recognize an end-grain board by the small sections of wood that make up the cutting surface. The board shown on page 66, custom made for me by the Bally Block Co., is not only an end-grain construction but is also dovetailed—the pieces are fitted together by interlocking joints.

The most common use for end-grain construction is butcher block, not butcher-block tabletops or cutting boards, but real butcher block that stands on legs, is 12 to 16 inches thick, 34 inches high, and weighs upward of 300 pounds. End-grain cutting boards are time-consuming and difficult to manufacture and are the most expensive of the three styles. They are heavy but extremely durable and warp-resistant, unless you really abuse them.

End-grain boards exact the smallest toll on your knife's edge compared to edge-grain and flat-grain boards. The wood fibers are pointed upward so you are cutting into them, not across them (much like placing a comb between bristles on a hairbrush) which helps your knife actually stay sharper longer. You are less likely to see knife marks on the board because the grain of the wood spreads to accommodate the blade, then reverts to its original form in a self-mending process.

An edge-grain board, seen on this page, is made from 2 x 4s turned so that the 2-inch side, or edge,

faces up. These boards are also strong and durable, and the best alternative to the end-grain variety if you don't want to pay the higher prices.

With proper care these boards will last for many, many years. Some of mine are marking their thirtieth anniversary. Edge-grain boards can be a very good value. They are generally not as thick as end grain, usually only 1 or 1¼ inches, but some companies do make a 3-inch variety.

Finally, if you turn that 2 x 4 so that you are looking at the 4-inch side, you have the makings of a flat-grain board, the weakest construction of the three, since only the smallest surface of that 2 x 4 is glued together. Even if the same quality wood, glue, and workmanship are used, these cutting boards are much more susceptible to warping at the ends, especially if you are not scrupulous about keeping them dry. Though I have several flat-grain boards, I prefer to spend the extra money for the more durable edge grain.

By far the majority of cutting boards produced by larger commercial board manufacturers are made from a variety of hard maple. Maple has the perfect properties for a cutting board. It is dense, close grained, uniformly textured, and has just the right hardness to be durable without quickly blunting your knife. There are soft maples that are about 25 percent softer than the hard varieties and not as well suited for the making of cutting boards, yet they are in use. Look for some designation—such as hard maple, rock maple, northern maple—that indicates a hard-maple product. There are companies that use other hardwoods such as cherry, white oak, birch, walnut, or a combination of these, and some even use exotic woods.

OTHER TYPES OF BOARDS

Bamboo

A recent and visually appealing addition to the cutting board scene is made from many laminated strips of bamboo, on page 69 at left. Bamboo is 16 percent harder than maple wood, weighs a third less than oak, yet in some instances is as strong as steel. When I was in China many years ago, bamboo was being used as scaffolding for building construction and I understand it is still used today. The species of bamboo used for cutting boards absorbs very little moisture and consequently does not shrink or swell as much as hardwoods.

Tom Sullivan of Totally Bamboo, one of the leading importers of bamboo boards, notes that bamboo cutting boards require the same care as other wood boards. The verdict is not yet in on whether the additional hardness of bamboo is as safe as maple for delicate knife edges. It is also not yet known how long the layers of laminated bamboo will hold together with repeated use. In addition, bamboo boards do not yet have the National Sanitation Foundation's stamp of approval, as do many wooden and plastic boards. They certainly have as much visual appeal as handcrafted wooden boards. Some of the strips are left in their natural color; some are steamed to darken the bamboo. This accounts for the spiffy-looking two-tone boards.

You can also find handmade, sometimes one-of-a-kind boards at juried craft fairs. Be sure to ask about the type of wood used, the board's suitability for food preparation, and the maintenance it will re-

quire. Also ask if the boards have been oiled and with what. If several different woods have been used, ask if they have the same density and expansion-shrinkage rate. These are all things you need to know.

Do not buy any cutting board that appears to have a high-gloss finish or film on it. The action of the knife on the board will cause the finish to flake and it may end up in your food.

Particle Board

Particle board is usually made from wood fragments (chips and shavings) that are bonded with resin, top right. The Snow River Wood Products company manufacturers a dishwasher-safe cutting board made from a high-density material that it claims "far exceeds the density of conventional particle board," to which they apply a top and bottom veneer. Since most people using this board will put it in the dishwasher after each use, there is little point in applying mineral oil.

Plastic

Plastic boards might be labeled as polyethylene, polypropylene, or just plain poly. These are all dishwasher safe, if that is your intention.

Before making a decision, rap the board with your knuckles. The louder the sound, the harder the board. These will take the greatest toll on your knife's edge. Consider the board if the rap produces a thud rather than a clunk. A board with very shiny, reflective surface is one to avoid. Some boards have a slightly textured surface, and I have found these to be kinder to my knife's edge when forced to use them.

Despite washing, some plastic boards tend to discolor with prolonged use. Carrot, red pepper, and parsley stains might be your constant companions. Finally, the number one reason I usually avoid plastic is that my knives just don't glide as well on plastic as they do on wood.

Hard Rubber

I have worked with hard rubber boards in several schools. The knife always seems to drag and I always find myself exerting more effort. Rubber boards are very heavy for their size and thickness and, if placed in the dishwasher, will warp with time. I have also noted a tendency for these boards to retain odors.

Glass, Marble, or Corian

I am distressed that these materials are being sold as cutting boards. All of these will dull your good knives immediately. Glass is also unsafe because your knife may slip while you are cutting. Marble is intended for use by bakers and pastry chefs who need a cool work surface. Corian, a DuPont polymer, is used primarily for countertops. Unless your goal is to dull the edge of your knife in a matter of seconds, do not use these products for cutting.

SELECTING A CUTTING BOARD

After you've decided on the type of grain you'd prefer, the next consideration should be size. Consider your available work space. If it is unlimited, purchase the largest board you can carry to the sink. Consider, too, the size of your longest chef's knife. Using a 10-inch blade on a 6-inch-wide board is a cramping experience. Your board size may also be limited if you have a galley-style kitchen. In that case, use the longest knife and deepest board you can manage with comfort. You might think about purchasing two boards—one large and one small board for tasks requiring only a paring or utility knife.

Also consider your height and the height of your counters. The standard height of a kitchen counter is 36 inches. Placing a 3-inch-thick cutting board on top of that is going to be quite uncomfortable for a shorter cook who will have to stretch up and raise her arm to cut. A taller person will have to bend or spread his stance to get lower. For most of your prep work, your elbow should be between the bottom of your rib cage and the top of your hip bone and almost never above midchest.

I'm 5 feet 4 inches and shrinking, and I had my worktable custom built so that the stand is 33 inches high and the edge-grain table surface is 6 feet x 3 feet x 2 inches. (I do not cut on this surface.) My biggest boards are 24 x 16 x 1¼ inches and 20 x 15½ x ½ inches. The smallest is 14 x 10 x ¾ inches. At the total height—table plus board—I am always comfortable when I prep.

You tall folks might consider a thick board. Remember, though, that thick boards are heavy. An 18 x 12 x 3-inch end-grain board can weigh almost 20 pounds. Go 20 x 15 x 3 inches and you're pressing about 25 pounds. 3-inch-high edge-grain boards will be lighter. For tall cooks, one of the advantages of a wood board over a plastic one is that you have the choice of different thicknesses. Plastic boards are usually no more than 1 inch thick. You might consider having a stable platform built to get your work surface raised. Your goal is to avoid having to stoop or spread your stance. It's rather difficult to make yourself shorter, so try to get your work surface to accommodate your height.

If you roast meat or poultry, consider a two-sided carving board. One side is routed around the outer edge to capture the juices from the roast, while the other side is a standard, flat cutting board. Consider

buying a board with routed handles such as the one shown above made by John Boos & Company. The grooved handles make for easy lifting to help me get those precious juices to the roasting pan or skillet where the sauce is being prepared.

If you are thinking about buying a board with little rounded plastic feet screwed in or glued at the corners, remember that the feet raise the board, so that must be taken into account when calculating the desired height of your work space. A footed board is a one-sided board—even if you unscrew the feet, the screw holes could harbor bacteria. All my cutting boards are two-sided—twice as much use from one board.

Finally, consider a board's aesthetic properties. Wood has the ability, like fine furniture, to age gracefully and acquire a warm and prized patina, if properly maintained. I have been told that used butcher blocks are worth more than new ones. Wood certainly has a lot more visual appeal than plastic, so once you discover how safe wood is to use, get the board or boards that best suit your needs and pocketbook.

MAINTAINING WOODEN BOARDS

You will have a better understanding of how to care for your wooden board if you know a little more about the product. Wood is a hygroscopic entity—it absorbs moisture from the air. Kiln-dried wood has a moisture content of 6 to 8 percent. It will absorb moisture and swell in high humidity, and release moisture and shrink in low humidity. This cycle occurs more frequently if the board lives in an area with distinct seasonal changes. The expansion occurs along the glued edges of the board. Don't worry—the glue expands too. Bally Board president James Reichart asserts that the growth can be as much as ½ inch in humid seasons. A move from Florida to Arizona will shrink your board. According to Reichart, the expansion-contraction cycle will diminish as the board gets older. It acclimates itself as it ages. The wood experts at upstate New York's Catskill Craftsmen, a wholesaler of boards and blocks, note that a board shipped to a drier climate may arrive slightly warped but that it will flatten itself out in a few days, once the moisture content finds its equilibrium.

With proper care, your wooden boards, particularly end- and edge-grain boards, will be passed on to the next generation. Here's how to make that happen:

• **Do not place wooden boards in the dishwasher.** The prolonged contact with water will swell the wood and the drying cycle will immediately shrink it. Wood does not like rapid changes in environment. If it dries too rapidly, the surface dries faster than the inside and results in separation and cracking. If for your own peace of mind (the germs!) you *must* use the dishwasher, use plastic boards instead of wooden ones, but note that prolonged heat often warps even plastic, so you will eventually have to discard it and buy a new one.

• **Do not leave wooden boards in the sink.** Wash your boards after each use with hot, soapy water; rinse and dry them immediately and thoroughly, including the edges. (I use paper towels for drying.)

Bacteria thrive on moisture and do not like an acidic environment. Joe Emerich of John Boos & Company states that, in addition to washing, a board can be further sanitized with a solution of 2 or

3 tablespoons vinegar to 2 cups water. Apply to the board's surface with a sponge, let it stand for several minutes, then rinse and dry thoroughly. You can also keep some plain white vinegar in a spray bottle for this purpose. I have also used a cut lemon as a sanitizer. Rub it on, let it sit a minute or two, rinse it off, then let it dry. Emerich discourages the use of any kind of bleach solution on wooden boards, though it is often used on plastic. Edmund Zottola of the University of Minnesota in Saint Paul notes that the organic structure of wood reacts with bleach, rendering it useless and "unavailable for killing germs." He concludes that "cooks have to be satisfied with just bathing their cutting boards." That would be a quick bath in hot, soapy water.

• **Keep boards away from moist or damp areas.** Avoid standing your board up against the sink's backsplash. After washing and drying, store boards in an upright position with separation between boards if you have more than one. Make sure the counter on which the board is resting is dry, because the ends are where most moisture enters and eventually warps and cracks the board, especially if it is flat grain. A seriously warped board should be discarded.

A board is considered cracked when gaps appear between the glued pieces. If the cracks (the technical terms is "checks") are in your cutting area, discard the board. It is a health hazard. If the cracks are at the very ends, the board may still be usable.

• **Keep boards away from any heat source.** Storing boards near a radiator can lead to excess shrinkage, and possibly warping and cracking.

• **Oil your board periodically.** Most boards come oil-finished from the manufacturer. One of the last production steps is to lower a rack of boards into a vat of some form of food-grade oil, lift them out, and let them hang to dry slowly. The truth is that a board's surface is never finished. Applying oil to the surface is an ongoing process for the life of the board. It will fill the wood's pores and make your cutting surface more impervious to food particles and liquids. It prevents food staining and also alleviates some of the expansion-shrinkage trauma as the board adapts to environmental humidity.

The old adage that a new board has to be oiled once a day for a week, once a week for a month, and once a month for a year sounds like a good rule, but it's not necessarily so. The manufacturers I spoke with suggested you apply at least one coat of oil before first use and periodically thereafter, usually once a week, depending on usage, board storage habits, and the humidity conditions in your house, particularly in the kitchen. No one confirmed the old adage, but you do have to be diligent. Check your new

will help protect your board and prolong its useful life. Do not use any kind of cooking oil—it will turn rancid. Food-grade mineral oil, found in the laxative section of your drugstore, is what I have been using for many years. It is an inexpensive, nontoxic petroleum derivative that does not require refrigeration. It does not offer lasting protection, but neither does anything else.

Al Ladd, a maker of specialty hardwood boards, recommends walnut oil, to which he also adds beeswax. I'm a bit leery of walnut oil, as it turns rancid easily. It should be stored in the refrigerator.

Almost every board manufacturer sells a proprietary oil and most of them are nothing more than mineral oil with beeswax or other additions, such as lemon oil. Beeswax adds a little more protection but is not a permanent solution. Regular washing of your boards requires periodic surface treatment, no matter what oil you use.

Do not oil your board immediately after washing and drying it. Let it air-dry for several hours or overnight. When ready, warm the oil in a pan set over low, direct heat for no more than 10 seconds. Depending on the size of the board, you'll need about 3 tablespoons for an 18 x 14-inch board, 2 tablespoons for a smaller one. End-grain boards will absorb more oil than edge- or flat-grain boards.

board—if it has a slight luster and feels smooth to the touch, it has been given an oil bath at the factory.

I recently purchased a board that looked light in color and also had a slightly grainy surface texture, a sure sign that it had not been thoroughly sanded at the factory. I gave it a gentle sanding, washed it, and dried it thoroughly. Several hours later I applied my own oil finish, repeating the application several times on both sides before putting it to use.

Repeated washing with soap and hot water will remove much of this oil finish. Oil darkens the board ever so slightly, so check for fading and a lack of surface luster as a sign that it's time to re-oil your board.

There are several readily available products that

Pour some oil on the board and rub it in with a soft cloth, following the grain. Be sure to oil all the way to the edges, especially the sides, where there is more moisture loss than on the cutting surface. Work the oil in, vigorously wipe off any excess, then allow the board to sit for several hours. If it is a two-sided board, remember which side you just oiled and, when time permits, do the other side.

SCORE MARKS

After prolonged use, you will begin to see score marks on your board especially in the area where you do most of your knife work. A one-piece maple board I picked up at a flea market for a pittance had what appeared to be a badly scored surface, see page 74. Actually, a quick brush of my hand revealed that the damage was superficial. At home, I gave it a light hand sanding with a medium grit (220 is fine) sandpaper, then oiled it. Score marks do not offend my sensibilities and the board is still in use after many years of faithful service. For illustration purposes, a coating of mineral oil was applied to the left side of the board before the picture was taken. Note the color difference.

GUNK

This 30-year-old flat-grain board, above, had been

sitting in my basement, alone and forsaken for many years. As an experiment, I decided to see if it could be put back into service. After thorough washing and drying, the surface still felt rather tacky so I gave it a thorough going-over with a stainless-steel bench scraper. Scraping removes much of the stickiness that can build up on a neglected wooden board.

It took a bit of doing, but eventually the tacky surface from the residue of old oil was removed. After sanding the board again with a medium-grit sandpaper, I washed and dried it thoroughly but did not oil it (for demonstration purposes)—note how pale and dry it looks. Several coats of mineral oil will restore the surface.

PART III

KNIFE
SKILLS

CHAPTER SEVEN

Basic Knife Techniques

Now that you have a good grasp of what the knives are, let's explore how to use them properly, efficiently, and painlessly. Many of my students admit that prepping for a meal often results in muscular stress, especially in the upper arm, shoulders, and neck. The truth is prepping does not have to be a chore.

GETTING A GRIP

Good knife skills begin with a correct grip. An incorrect one will cause unnecessary muscle tension and with it, fatigue and frustration. You are probably willing to pay a lot of money to have your golf or tennis grip improved. Why not think of your knife in the same way? You use it almost every day. In that respect, the knife is no different from any other tool. Grip a hammer, screwdriver, wooden spoon, or wire whisk in a way that does not give you the most efficient motion and all those tools become unnecessarily difficult to use. We'll start with the 8- and 10- inch knives as they require a grip that is different from the one used on smaller knives. At this point you might want to review the parts of the knife (see page 20), as they will be referenced often in this chapter.

The handle of the knife is the first thing that greets your hand when you start your prep work. How you greet your knife will determine how effective and tension-free your prep session will be.

Pinch the sides of the heel just above the bolster with your thumb and forefinger. The second joint of your index finger or thereabouts should be resting just above the spine of the knife and should be lifted enough so it is out of the way of the blade edge. Gently curl the remaining three fingers around the handle with your middle finger placed up against the finger guard. There should be no gap between the handle and your palm, and the back of your hand should be facing up. This grip allows for the greatest freedom of movement. Remember to keep your shoulder down and your wrist flexible. Avoid clenching the handle like a hammer, holding the handle near the butt, or placing the thumb or index finger on the spine of the blade (although this position is sometimes useful), as all of these grips lead to unnecessary arm and wrist tension.

If the bolster does not have a finger guard or choil, pinching the heel with the thumb and forefinger and the subsequent wrap around the handle will still give you the correct grip.

If you have long fingers and the grip on a standard blade feels cramped, consider a blade with a wider heel such as those made by Wüsthof and Messermeister.

If you want your prep work to be as tension-free as possible, it is essential that you give up the tight grip. Over the years I have observed this tendency to grip the knife handle too tightly—I have seen white knuckles from across the room—even after the proper grip has been mastered.

In thinking about the problem, I came to the realization that many of you have assumed, observed, or learned that the proper way to cut is to press straight down with some part of the knife. Perhaps there is also the assumption that a tight grip assures control. I believe just the opposite to be true.

One of the first things many students do when they settle in at their cutting boards is pick up the chef's knife and place the tip on the board while pressing the heel straight down. The knife is not an axe that requires blunt downward or sideward force to do its job. Instead it works best when it glides

"The most perfect technique is that which is not noticed at all."

—Pablo Casals

through as it is pushed or pulled, not simply pressed downward or laterally, which merely crushes whatever you are tying to cut. If I were to compare the knife to any tool it would be to the handsaw not the axe. Clenching the handle and exerting downward force results in tension and that's what you want to avoid.

To self-test the tight grip and become aware of the tension it creates, grip the chef's knife or any long knife using the proper technique described above. Lightly circle your wrist with your free hand and tighten the grip on the handle. You will feel the muscles tighten. Repeat this exercise while circling

the bicep of your knife arm with your free hand. Again you will feel your muscle tighten. The tight grip is the hardest habit for new students to become aware of and overcome, because it is so deeply ingrained in the muscle memory from years of use. If you are having tension problems in a sport, you know that changing muscle habits takes understanding, concentration, and lots of repetition, to make the necessary changes. The same goes for knife skills.

I have had students tell me they know their grip is too tight but they just can't break the habit. I hope that by practicing the techniques in this section you will become aware of the white-knuckle syndrome and its effects on everything you try to cut. Ultimately, you are the only one who can recognize and alter this habit.

The Other Hand

I'm sure you are aware from watching cooking shows or someone who has good knife skills, that slicing and dicing requires two hands. The other hand is often referred to as the guide hand or, as I shall refer to it, the holding hand. Its purpose is both to hold the food down and to guide the knife so that your pieces are evenly cut and thus evenly cooked. There are several ways to shape the holding hand, depending on the object being cut.

Fingers Closed

· Form a circle with the thumb and index finger making sure that the thumb is placed behind the index finger for safety reasons.

· Curl the remaining fingers so that they line up with the index finger. Note that the middle finger extends beyond the others.

· Curl the first joints slightly under. The middle joint of the middle finger should be at a right angle to the cutting board. This is the knife's guide and stopper. Hold the arm as though it were in a sling—knife and holding hands should now be perpendicular.

· Gently place the pads of the fingers on the item being cut. Keep the fingers together and relaxed. Before you pick up the knife, practice by placing the holding hand in the fingers-closed position on the cutting board, holding the arm as though it were a sling. Creep the thumb back ¼ inch, then bring the other fingers back to meet the thumb. Repeat several times until it begins to feel natural.

· Place the palm of the knife hand against the holding hand and keep it there as it moves to the left (or right). This coordinated motion takes some practice but is well worth the effort. If you have learned to tap your head and rub your belly at the same time, you can do this.

· Now try this holding the chef's knife. Place the flat side of the blade up against the middle joint of your middle finger and move the blade forward and backward, keeping the knife on the board. At this point fear can often take over. You think you are going to cut yourself, but I guarantee that you won't. You can rub the knife against that middle finger all day long and will not cut yourself as long as you maintain the proper holding-hand and knife positions.

· Creep the holding hand to the left or right, keeping the blade in contact with the middle finger. As soon as the knife has crossed the center of your body, move the food back to the starting position. Repeat several times until it begins to feel natural. When you actually start cutting real food, don't try for speed or become obsessive about evenly sized pieces at first.

For those still not quite ready to place the flat side of the knife against the fingers, place the holding hand on top of the food you are cutting, about 2 inches from the end. (Placing your guide hand too far from the knife creates instability. Your food item can wobble, making it difficult to achieve evenly sized pieces.) Slowly push the food toward the stationary knife and reposition your holding hand when necessary.

Here are some common mistakes people make with the holding hand:

1. Making a fist with the thumb tucked inside (probably to protect the fingernails) and knuckles very close to the board.

2. Extending the fingers almost flat against the item you are trying to cut.

3. Tucking the fingers under and having your thumb extend beyond your knuckles.

These mistakes leave the knuckles, fingertips, or thumb exposed to the oncoming blade and an almost certain (but avoidable) accident. The knife has no conscience—it will cut whatever it encounters first.

Fingers Open

Use this position to stabilize whole, large, round fruits and vegetables, like onions, tomatoes, and eggplants.

· Curl the fingers as for the fingers-closed grip.

· In the center of the object to be sliced, spread the fingers across the top half so the thumb and pinky are on opposite sides and the remaining fingers are spaced across the top.

· Creep the fingers back to get the desired thickness.

Fingers Bunched

Used this position to slice or mince small items such as garlic, leeks, or shallots. This position is similar to the fingers-closed grip except that all the fingers are bunched around the thumb. The middle finger is still the stopper. The arm is still in the sling position.

The No-Roll Hold

Use this position to cut a whole carrot or anything that could roll as the knife makes contact.

· Place the index finger on top of the item with the second joint at a right angle to the food—this is the stopper. Thumb and middle finger are slightly behind the index finger on opposite sides of the item. The back of the item is lightly held in place by your palm.

· Creep the hand back with each stroke of the knife for the next cut.

The Palm-on-Top Hold

Use this position to cut bagels and rolls, butterfly cuts of meat, and get those last few slices from large, round fruits and vegetables.

· Place the whole palm directly on top of the item you are cutting.

· With the knife positioned parallel to the board, push forward for bagels, rolls, and sheet cakes, or pull for chicken breasts and chops.

The Arc Hold

Use this technique for greater stability when cutting a carrot or shallot in half lengthwise or making that last pull near the thumb of the holding hand.

· Hold the thumb and the middle, or several fingers on either side of the item.

· Place the knife through the arc and make an angled cut either by pushing or pulling.

These are the basic positions of the guide hand. Others will be introduced as we work through the various techniques. You may even discover your own comfortable positions. In the next section you'll put it all together using the chef's knife.

KNIFE POSITIONS

Almost everything that needs to be prepped in the average kitchen can be done using just a few positions of this knife. These positions are not exclusive to the chef's knife but can also be used with the carving, paring, and utility knife.

Perpendicular

Much of what you normally cut, whether it is ½ or 5 inches thick, uses this position, in which the blade is held perpendicular to the board. There are different techniques for cutting low and high items but the 90-degree angle that the knife forms with the board does not change. The blade is either angled down to push or up (tip higher than handle) to pull.

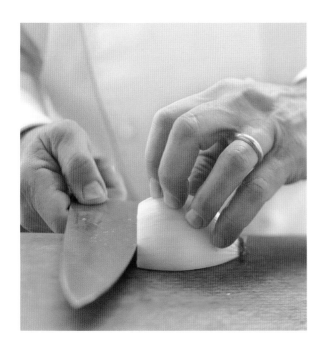

Parallel

In this position the blade is held parallel to the board. Your knuckles face outward for this one, as for the palm-on-top hold (see page 84). It is used when dicing onions, getting those last few slices, and removing the spongy portion of bell peppers. With other knives, the parallel position is used for cutting fruits, bagels, and rolls; for cutting Italian-style bread in half for sandwiches; and for cutting sponge and sheet cakes into layers. The knife is placed against the item being cut with the tip pointing straight ahead and is pushed forward, never laterally, with slight pressure, towards the holding hand. At the end of the push, pull the knife back in the groove just cut and repeat this motion, which might best be described as a zigzag.

Angled

In this position the blade is placed at a 45-degree angle to the item. It is used for cutting meat and vegetables on the bias, as in the photo at left.

CUTTING STANCE

Before doing any actual cutting, you and your board need to get in the proper position. To get the best elliptical motion from the knife arm, stand back 7 or 8 inches from the cutting board. If you're too close to the board, you will feel cramped and could clamp your upper arm to your ribs—not a good thing to do when you are trying to achieve a relaxed and fluid motion. You should have 3 to 4 inches of space between your elbow and your rib cage. If you're too close to the board, you will also have to place the item being cut at the center or far edge of the board, which, when you're using smaller knives, causes your knuckles to hit the board. You will want to have the food item 2 to 3 inches from the front of the cutting board and centered. The board should be flush with the front edge of your worktable.

Parallel Stance/Angled Knife

Stand with your torso parallel to the board, feet under your shoulders, so you feel centered and balanced. Angle the knife slightly to the left if you are right-handed. The tip of the knife points toward the center of the far edge of the board. To get a straight cut, angle the food to keep it and the knife at right angles.

Angled Stance/Knife Straight Ahead

Stand at a 45-degree angle to the board, facing right or left, and plant your feet squarely under your shoulders. Hold the knife parallel to the side of the board, tip pointing straight ahead. To get a straight cut, angle the food to keep it and the knife at right angles.

No matter which stance you choose, avoid excessive arm angles—the tip of the knife facing the far corner—that create upper-arm and shoulder tension.

CUTTING LOW AND HIGH ITEMS

Once you determine which cutting stance is most comfortable and which knife position is best suited for the job, you need to decide whether the item you are cutting is low or high. A stalk of celery is low; an onion, potato, or a grapefruit is high. Low items require a very different technique from high items. Ask yourself these questions to be sure you are using the correct technique for each.

1. Where is the tip of the knife placed at the start of the cut?

Low: on the board.

High: on top of the item, a little ahead of the item being cut, tip angled down.

2. Is the knife pushed or pulled to do the cutting?

Low: pushed away from you.

High: pushed away from you; as the tip reaches the board, begin decreasing the angle of the blade until it is flush with the board.

3. What part and how much of the blade is needed to do the cutting?

Low: only the back half (or less) of the blade.

High: a longer portion of the blade, using the same forward-downward motion.

4. How is the knife repositioned for the next cut?

Low: handle is lifted and tip is dragged back to start the next cut.

High: blade is lifted straight up, angled, and put into motion before it makes contact with the top of the item.

The Low Technique

In the low technique, some part of the blade edge is on the cutting board at all times and the tip never tilts up. In the starting position, the tip is placed on the board and the heel is raised. In the end position, the flat of the blade is flush with the board and the tip is pointed straight ahead.

Depending on the length of the blade used, the actual cutting is done between the middle and the heel of the blade, not near the tip. The forward-downward stroke brings the back half of the knife flush to the board. After what you are cutting has been separated from the main piece, the forward motion continues until the heel of the blade reaches the food item. That is called follow-through. It is not a full stop, an action that will flex the biceps. Immediately after the follow-through, without stopping the motion, the handle is raised high enough to clear the item being cut and, at the same time, the tip is pulled back along the board to start the swooplike, forward-downward process again for the next cut. The handle lift and pullback are one motion.

This is really a continuous, elliptical sequence of motions, not a push-stop-pull-stop sequence. Stopping tenses the upper arm and interrupts the flow. Sounds easy but it's not. Practice the motion first without cutting any food. Then place a low item, such as a stalk of celery, on the board.

The techniques described next require that the knife be pushed, not pulled to make the actual cut. Pulling is a legitimate technique that is used in special circumstances. I have observed that those who belong to the "I don't use anything larger than a steak knife" school of cutting have a difficult time making the transition to the push method. In most cases, the forward-pushing motion is a more efficient use of arm and shoulder strength than pulling backward. I'm going to assume that you have at least an 8-inch chef's knife. Do not attempt this technique with anything smaller.

1. Put the celery 3 to 4 inches from the front edge of your board, either angled or straight according to your preferred stance.

2. Place the tip of the knife on the board with the heel directly over the celery with the holding hand in place.

3. Raise and pull the knife back until you reach the center of the blade.

4. Push the knife forward as you lower it gradually (forward and down—not down and forward, the dreaded press-down technique), separating the celery slice from the stalk gradually as the back half of the knife meets the board and glides forward. The tip of the blade is now raised off the board due to the curve of the blade, and the rest of the edge or the back half is on the board.

5. Continue the forward, gliding motion until the bolster is near the food item. This is the follow-through, which completes the separation of the slice from the main item and relaxes the upper arm.

6. At the very end of the follow-through, without stopping the motion, lift the handle and drag the tip back until the knife is centered over the celery again, move the holding hand, and immediately make the next cut.

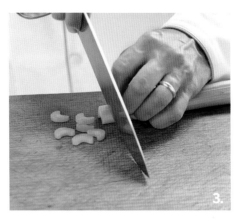

Learning a new series of muscle movements is difficult and takes time and practice, so please be patient. In my classes, I have three hours to change long-standing muscle memory habits. You have the rest of your life.

Using a Longer Chef's Knife

If you used an 8-inch chef's knife for the celery exercise, try the same technique of cutting something low with a 10-inch knife. The sequence of movements used with the 8-inch knife does not change. You still place the tip on the board, and push and make the cut with a forward-downward motion and a follow-through. But when you raise the handle and pull back on the tip to return to your starting position, you will raise and pull the knife back until you reach the last 3 to 4 inches rather than the center of the blade, then continue the forward, gliding motion until the bolster reaches the food item.

The photos at right show a side-by-side comparison.

When you cut a low item with the 8-inch knife, you need the back half of the blade to make the cut and follow through. If you start the cut too far back on the blade, you will run out of room and instinctively press down. If you start the cut nearer to the tip, you will have to raise your elbow higher

than necessary and create side-muscle stress. The beauty of the 10-inch blade is that its extra 2 inches of length also provide additional heft. It permits the cutting of small pieces much farther back on the blade where there is more weight. It is not efficient to cut something 1 inch wide with 5 or 6 inches of blade. You need at most 3 inches, and since you have more weight to work with, your muscles will have to work less. Finally, since the blade is longer, you have more options as to how much blade to use, whether to use a long stroke or a short stroke, for example. Smaller items require less of the blade. This is true for both 8- and 10-inch blades. If your item is wider, the longer blade has a clear advantage. You have fewer options with shorter knives. With practice you will figure out exactly how much blade is necessary to make the cut and get a proper follow-through.

The High Technique

The extra length and weight that are helpful when cutting low items are equally useful in dealing with high items, such as potatoes, onions, peppers, and pineapples. I use a large, well-tapered carrot in class to demonstrate the difference between the two techniques. The tip of the carrot and maybe the first half can be cut using the low technique. As the girth increases, however, trying to keep the tip of the knife on

the board begins to cause stress—your elbow starts to raise to armpit height, the side muscles stretch upward, and your shoulder hunches forward.

Earlier I compared a knife to a handsaw—both are angled down, cut on the push, and are pulled back to continue cutting with another push. The full length of the handsaw is utilized to achieve the cut. Perpendicular cutting is done with the tip of the knife angled up or down, and always down when pushing. Sometimes the knife is kept in the groove that has just been cut, sometimes a new cut is made. Even low items are cut at an angle. As soon as you have the tip on the board and the handle raised, the knife is automatically angled downward. It straightens out just before the follow-through. If the importance of pushing at a downward angle escaped you as you learned and practiced the low technique, the lesson on the high technique will give you another chance. Review the questions and answers on page 89-91, now that you have learned the low technique, to see how the high technique differs.

In the high technique, the tip is not placed on the board but on top of and a little ahead of the item to be cut, and it is angled downward. The knife is pushed until the tip reaches or is near the board. The handle is lowered gradually and the angle of the blade decreases until it is flush with the board. During this motion, do not press down on the handle and allow the tip of the knife to come up so the spine is parallel to the board. The moment that happens, you will have to press down to complete the cut.

Compared to the low technique, the high technique requires a longer portion of the blade to make the cut, but it uses the same forward-downward motion as the low technique. The more blade you use, the better you can follow through, and the less tension you produce in the upper arm because you are using proper technique instead of pressing down.

At the end of the follow-through, while the blade is still moving forward, the knife is lifted straight up off the board while the holding hand is moved back the desired distance. The blade is angled and brought back to the starting position and the forward-downward motion is repeated for the next cut before the knife makes contact with the food item.

There is a tendency to press down with the tip to start each cut. Don't! Any strictly downward force of the knife creates tension in the grip and upper arm. To get a fluid, repetitive motion, start the cut with the knife already moving forward. As you bring the knife up, back and angled, start the forward motion when the tip is close to, but not on the food. Trust me—with practice, you'll be able to master this movement and

feel how the fluid motion increases the ease and effectiveness of your cutting.

Before you try this with knife in hand, simulate the motion with your holding hand in place and your open palm acting as the knife. If you need a high-technique mantra try, "Forward and down, glide and follow through, lift, back and angle, move holding hand, cut again."

Adjusting for Different Heights

A carrot is not a potato is not a pineapple. The starting downward angle of the knife does not increase in direct proportion to the height of the item you are cutting. If your elbow is above your chin, you're not doing this correctly. To achieve height for this technique, raise and angle the blade with your forearm rather than your elbow. Above, from left to right, are sample positions for a carrot, a potato, a large onion, and a pineapple. Note that the angle of the blade remains fairly consistent, and that the forearm and elbow maintain their angle as the blade is raised. The only thing that changes is the size of the object being cut. Going back to the handsaw analogy, after you make your pushed and angled cut, you pull the saw back in the groove you have just made, then push again at the same angle, thus cutting deeper and deeper into the board until it is separated. High food items are cut the same way. It is not always possible to make the desired cut in one motion, even if you have that wonderful 10-inch chef's knife.

When cutting a large onion, eggplant, or cabbage, you may run out of blade halfway or two-thirds of the way down. Instead of the technique you used on the carrot, pull the knife back in the cut you have already made, leaving an inch or so

 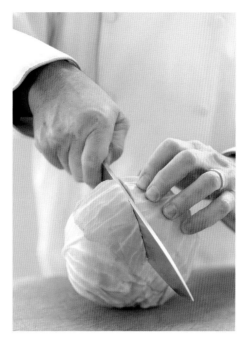 

of blade exposed on the far side of the item, then push forward and down again, keeping the angle constant. The blade only straightens out as you near the board, then follow through. See the cabbage photos above, at right.

It's better to make two or three of these sawlike cuts than one press down motion. This is not about bravado—who can cut that onion in one stroke— but rather about having a relaxed, fluid technique.

How will you know when you are using the correct technique? Your elbow and upper arm positions as well as your side muscles will send you signals. If your shoulder is pushed into your neck and your elbow is parallel to your ears, you are using the wrong technique. Don't try to cut something high using the low position. The length of your knife is important to consider, too: a 10-inch blade will handle the low position better than an 8-inch one can.

PULLING A KNIFE

All the work so far has been done with the knife being pushed away from your body to do the cutting, with the knife angled downwards. But sometimes it is not possible to push, for example when you need to cut something into vertical strips and still keep them attached at one end, as above. You'll need this technique to dice an onion and fan a strawberry, among other things.

For the chef's knife, the following technique will primarily be applied to onions. Observe the positions of the knife at above.

Place the heel of the knife at the front edge of the onion—heel down, tip up. Maintaining the angle, pull the knife back and down. Without stopping your motion, raise the handle to pull the tip from the back of the board to the front making sure you feel the tip on the board throughout the movement. Pull the tip off the board to follow through, and without stopping, return to the starting position and repeat.

Mastering the techniques described above will enable you to tackle the majority of food items in your prep sessions. Determining which items are low and which are high, which need pushing and which need pulling will eventually become second nature.

CUTTING ASIAN STYLE

Many Asian recipes call for meats and vegetables to be cut on the bias. This type of cut exposes more surface area to the heat, so the item cooks quickly. Many of the Chinese cabbages, especially those in the bok choy family, are cut this way, as are chicken breast, pork, flank steak, and fish fillets. Even celery can be cut this way for salads or Asian-style dishes. Hard, solid vegetables such as carrots should be cut on the bias with the knife in the perpendicular position.

Either a chef's knife or carving knife may be used—the longer the knife, the easier the task. The key to mastering this technique is to avoid pressing down with the knife at the start of the cut. For the depth, place the tip of the knife at the starting point with your fingers over the blade edge. With a very low angle (about 10 degrees) and almost no downward pressure, push forward until the tip meets the board, then pull to separate, keeping the tip on the board. The thickness of the slice is determined by the knife's angle. A high angle yields thick pieces and less surface area, a low angle yields thin pieces and more surface area. Your fingers are insulated by the slice you are cutting.

LEARNING TO DICE

At some point in your culinary life you are going to have to dice something—potatoes for a chowder, vegetables in a consommé (a clear, light broth). A true dice results in cubes that are the end product of a series of several other important cuts. You can cut any size dice you want as long as the slices and strips are cut to the correct thickness. Before starting to dice, look for guidance from the recipe. Hopefully it will give you the size of the dice—⅛-inch or 1 inch—because that will determine the size of the other cuts you'll have to make. I use the terms small, medium, or large when referring to dice. If the ingredient needs to be a specific size, I provide the measurement. If the size is too small to measure then it is commonly called a mince. (One dices onions but minces shallots.) If no measurement is given, use common sense.

>> Everybody complains about food sticking to the knife, but you can use this to your advantage. Line up a stuck slice or strip with the outer edge of the next cut to get evenly sized pieces.

Round and Semiround Items

This technique can be used for round or semiround items, such as potatoes, turnips, or eggplant, but we'll use a potato as an example. Once peeled, it must be cut in such a way that you end up with all sides parallel, and that's not as easy as it sounds. For a true dice, the ends and the sides of the item are going to be wasted.

1. Place the potato near the right (or left) side of your board and use the board's edge to keep your cuts straight and parallel.

2. Using a chef's knife and the high technique, remove both ends where the potato's curve stops.

3. Stand the potato on one of the flat ends and remove the curved sides in four cuts to form a large block, trying to keep opposing cuts parallel.

4. Decide what size dice you want (for ¼-inch dice, cut ¼-inch slices and so on) and, using the high technique, cut the slices to the desired thickness.

5. Stack two or three slices (be careful not to stack them too high—they could slip) and, using the low technique, cut the strips to the desired thickness. Turn the strips horizontally and cut crosswise to dice using the low technique.

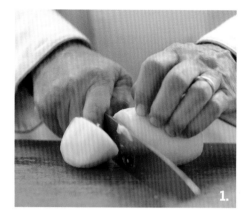

1.

2.

3A.

3B.

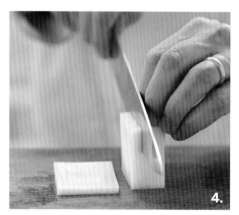

4.

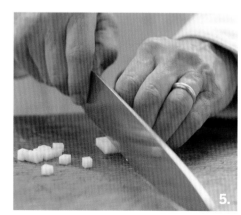

5.

Round Tapered Items

This technique can be used for round tapered items, such as carrots or parsnips. The same sequence of cuts used for the potato is used here but with one essential difference—you can't block the entire carrot because of its taper. If you need strips cut to a specified length, then that's your guide. If the length of the strips is not your main consideration, cut the longest segment you can manage from the root end. If the carrot is thick enough, you might be able to cut another block and get more slices, strips, or dice from it.

1. Peel the carrot and cut a 3- or 4-inch piece from the root end. Stand the carrot upright on the wider flat end and, using the high technique, remove the curved sides in four cuts to form a block, trying to keep opposing cuts parallel. Another method is to cut off one rounded side, then place the carrot flat-side down to remove the other three.

2. Decide what size dice you want (for a $\frac{1}{4}$-inch dice, cut $\frac{1}{4}$-inch slices and so on) and, using the high technique, cut the slices to the desired thickness.

3. Using the low technique, cut the strips to the desired thickness.

4. Turn the strips horizontally cut crosswise to dice using the low technique.

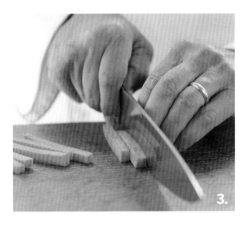

CUTTING WITH PARING AND UTILITY KNIVES

While the chef's knife usually employs one basic grip, the smaller paring or utility knife requires you to use a variety of grips depending on how you will be using it. For knives 6 inches or smaller, all the cutting needs to be at the near edge of the board. Placing the item in the middle or at the far edge will result in your knuckles pressing into the board and raising the blade edge off the board.

The All-Purpose Grip

The following grip, seen at left, used for cutting fruits or slicing and mincing garlic or shallots, works for both the paring and the utility knife and is intended for making perpendicular or parallel cuts either pushing or pulling.

If you use the same grip as with a chef's knife, your index finger or knuckles will hit the board as you try to guide the blade forward, preventing a good follow-through. This all-purpose grip keeps your fingers away from the heel of the knife and allows you to use the whole blade.

Place the index finger on top of the bolster, with the thumb and middle finger right behind it on opposite sides of the handle. Support the back of the handle with last two fingers, resting the butt in the lower palm.

The Peeling Grips

For any outer skins that need to be peeled, curl the last three fingers around the handle with the blade facing the fingertips. Place the index finger loosely underneath the heel, close to the bolster. The blade can then be inserted under the skin of the item, starting at the upper right or left corner. The thumb is clamped over the skin which is pulled towards the root or base. This technique is most commonly used with the paring knife but can also be used with the utility knife for medium-size items like shallots, or the chef's knife for large items like onions.

For peeling round fruits and vegetables, cup the handle with four fingers, blade angled down. Place the thumb on the near side of the item being peeled. The blade can be straight or angled depending on the item. Rotate the item toward the knife with the holding hand.

The Snippy Grip

This grip, what I like to call "grandma's grip," is similar to the peeling grip and is used for slicing string beans, bananas, celery, or anything that is small enough to fit between the knife blade and your thumb. Cup the handle with four fingers, blade edge facing your thumb, and pull the blade toward your thumb to make the cut. Do not move the blade up or down across your thumb. This grip can be done using a paring knife or a 5- to 6-inch utility knife.

The Scraping Grip

This grip, used for removing the skin from ginger or making garlic puree, is similar to the peeling grip but the knife makes a scraping rather than a slicing motion, and the spine rather than the edge of the knife does the work.

To scrape the skin off ginger, cup the knife handle with four fingers, blade facing up, and scrape from bottom to top with the spine of the blade.

To make garlic puree, support the handle with four fingers. Place the index finger on the heel with the blade facing away from you and angled up at about 45 degrees. Scrape across and down over the rounded surface with the spine of the blade. Follow through and repeat.

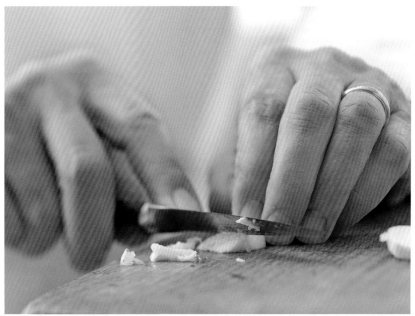

The Coring Grip

To core tomatoes or strawberries, or remove bruised areas of fruit, hold the tip of the pairing knife with the thumb and index fingers—thumb across the first joint of the index finger to form a 90-degree angle, index finger at the bottom of the thumbnail—with the blade facing the fingertips. Rest the spine against the base of the remaining fingers with the bolster at or near the base of the pinky finger. Gently curl the remaining fingers to support the spine and handle. (You cannot cut yourself unless you press extraordinarily hard, and there is no reason to do that.) The amount of the tip showing above the thumb will determine the depth of the core being removed—more for a tomato, less for a strawberry, even less for the eye of a potato.

You might want to practice the coring technique without the knife at first. Simulate the coring grip with your knife hand and, with the thumbnail facing up, push your thumb into the center of the palm of your holding hand, as though you were removing a core from the center of your palm. Keep your thumb in place as you rotate the knife hand toward you so the back of your knife hand is facing up.

Rotate your knife hand back to the starting position (thumbnail up) as you simultaneously turn the holding hand in the opposite direction (toward you). Do this several times until it begins to feel natural.

When you do this technique with the knife, never remove your thumb from the top of the core until you have made a complete circle around the core (usually two or three turns), at which point the knife and core can be pulled out. This prevents the knife from slipping and cutting you.

The quality of the knives you choose for your wardrobe, the way you prep them and the motions you use to cut will determine whether your prep sessions are stressful or not.

Chef's knives employ one basic grip whether cutting low or high items or whether used in the perpendicular, parallel, or angled positions.

These same positions are used with the smaller knives but the grip changes according to what is being cut. Note that in the techniques that follow, the low technique is not used with the small knives—the blades are too short.

As you work through these techniques, observe both grip and holding hand positions. Add the proper cutting motions and, with practice, your prep sessions will be cut in half.

CHAPTER EIGHT

Preparing Fruits and Vegetables

The fruits and vegetables in this chapter will require many of the techniques you have learned so far. The suggested knives should be seriously considered, as your goal is to prep with minimal stress and tension. I generally recommend longer, heavier knives for tackling big vegetables. Where a chef's knife is indicated in the techniques that follow, I would use the 10-inch variety but in many cases an 8-inch will also work. You'll get very discouraged trying to shred cabbage with a 6-inch utility knife. Forget about slicing rutabagas.

Slicing usually connotes a forward motion, that is, the knife is being pushed away from you. There are times, however, when it is more efficient to pull the knife toward you. The end result of slicing is to separate a segment from the whole.

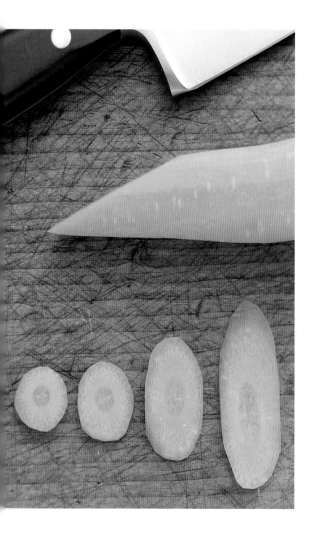

When you realize that a slice can be further cut into thick or thin strips and those strips cut crosswise into a dice of any size or a mince, you begin to understand and appreciate how basic slicing is. I will use the term *slice* when any of the above techniques are employed and the word *cut* if other methods are used. Some strips have French names that indicate precise measurements—the *julienne* is a ⅛- x ⅛-inch matchstick cut 1 to 2 inches long. The *bâtonnet* is a ¼- x ¼-inch stick cut to 2 or 2½ inches. Cut the julienne crosswise into a dice and it is called a *brunoise*. I like recipes that indicate the size of the slice, strip, or dice required.

Note the omission of the word *chop*, a technique that involves a striking blow done from above with a heavy knife or cleaver and a very flexible wrist. Despite the common use of the word, most prep work does not require chopping. The knife is not a blunt-force instrument. It cuts most effectively when it is pushed or pulled.

CUTTING THINGS EVENLY

In order for cut items to cook evenly, they must be cut into evenly sized pieces. Many years ago I took a baking class with Nick Malgieri at The New School in New York. I watched him take a stick of butter out of the wrapper, cut it in half, then cut each half in half again, until he had eight perfectly equal tablespoon segments each weighing ½ ounce. He needed six tablespoons—three ounces—and did not use the guides on the wrapper, or start cutting at one end. I learned from that demonstration how important it is to cut things evenly. Decide in advance what the size of your pieces is going to be. If you make a mistake or change your mind, get another fruit or vegetable and start over. Do not try to fix the existing slices or crush them into smaller pieces—they'll never be evenly sized and will not cook evenly. This concept will be mentioned frequently in the techniques that follow.

Recipes call for many different types of cuts from vegetables. To change the angle at which an item is cut, keep the knife in the standard position and rotate the item from a 90-degree angle for a straight cut to 45-degrees or less for a bias cut, shown at left.

Dice

FRUIT OR VEGETABLE: CELERY
KNIFE: CHEF'S KNIFE

Trim both ends of the stalk and place vertically on the board, rounded-side up.

1. Place the tip of the knife about an inch past the far end of the stalk and make a forward cut 2 to 3 inches in length. Note the holding hand position.

2. When the tip of the knife is on the board, bring the knife back to where the previous cut ended and make another forward cut.

3. Continue in this fashion until the heel of the knife is over the near end of the stalk. Glide forward and down to complete the split.

4. Crosscut these halves for a large dice. For a smaller dice, cut each half in half again lengthwise and crosscut. You can use the same technique to cut the stalk into three equal parts. The size of the strips and the crosscut determines the final dice.

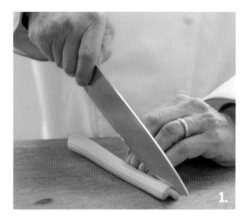

Julienne

FRUIT OR VEGETABLE: CELERY
KNIFE: CHEF'S KNIFE

The julienne's measurements—$\frac{1}{8}$ x $\frac{1}{8}$-inch—assumes that you are able to cut your food item into perfect cubes, which is not always the case when the food item in question is not a perfect square. But where there's a will, there's a method.

Use the thicker, outer stalks of the celery for this technique. Trim both ends of the stalk and place horizontally on the board.

1. Cut the celery into $2\frac{1}{2}$- to 3-inch-long pieces.

2. Cut each piece in half lengthwise.

3. Place each half horizontally on the board and use the parallel technique (page 87) and the last 3 or 4 inches of the knife to cut the pieces in half. Keep the holding hand ahead of the oncoming knife.

4. Place the curved half on top and use the low technique to cut the julienne.

Noncubed Dice

FRUIT OR VEGETABLE: CARROTS AND OTHER TAPERED VEGETABLES
KNIFE: CHEF'S KNIFE

True dicing results in cubes, but many soups or braised dishes do not require a perfect cube—a quarter-round cut will do very well.

1. Cut the carrot in half crosswise.

2. Cut the thicker half in half lengthwise or in quarters, depending on the final size you want. (Note the arc hold.)

3. Place flat-side down. Cut across to get the final size. Then cut the thinner half in half lengthwise.

4. Place flat side down. Cut across and try to match the final size from the thicker half as best you can.

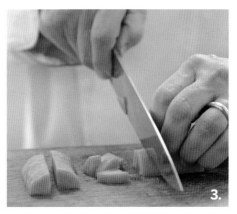

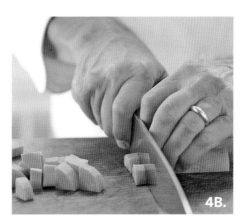

Quarters

FRUIT OR VEGETABLE: CABBAGE
KNIFE: CHEF'S KNIFE

The following techniques work for green, red, or Savoy cabbages.

You'll need the high technique and a true sawing motion for this cut because you will most likely not be able to quarter a head of cabbage in one stroke. You may run out of blade halfway or two-thirds of the way through the cut.

1. Place the knife in the high position and make the first cut.

2. Pull the knife back in the cut you have already made, leaving an inch or so of blade exposed at the tip.

3. Push forward and down again and repeat as necessary. The blade should straighten out only when you are very near the board, then you follow through.

4. Place the halved cabbage flat-side down and use the high technique to cut into quarters.

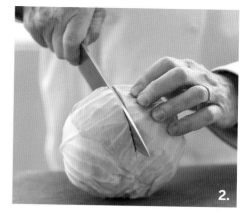

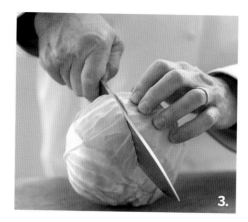

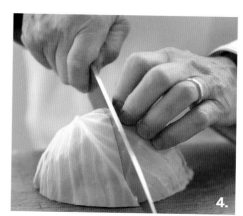

Shred

FRUIT OR VEGETABLE: CABBAGE
KNIFE: CHEF'S KNIFE

Now that you have the cabbage quartered, you need to remove the core.

1. Place the cabbage core-side down and remove the core following its angle.

2. Place the cored cabbage flat-side down at about a 45-degree angle and, with the high technique, cut thick or thin shreds.

3. You can also remove several layers of leaves and cut them into shreds using the low technique.

ONIONS

There are several techniques for cutting onions. Some are single-step cuts, such as rings, some are a series of cuts as for diced onions. No matter which technique you are using, your knife must be sharp. If you crush this delicate creature, you will pay with tears. For many of the techniques I write about you must be able to distinguish between the root end and the stem end (in the picture below, the stem end is on the left). Also note the different grips employed.

> ## "Mine eyes smell onions: I shall weep anon."
>
> **—from *All's Well that Ends Well* by William Shakespeare**

Why You Cry

Onion cells contain two sections separated by a membrane—one section contains an enzyme, the other sulfur compounds. When the onion is cut, the enzyme and sulfur compounds combine to form a mild sulfuric acid. The acid reaches your tear ducts, which produce more water to dilute the irritating substance.

Cold temperatures will slow the enzymatic reaction, so try putting the onion in the refrigerator for 30 to 45 minutes before cutting it. You will also find that using a sharp knife to cut the onion can greatly reduce your tears as the cell walls are cleanly cut rather than crushed.

Peeling Onions

FRUIT OR VEGETABLE: ONIONS
KNIFE: 3½-INCH PARING KNIFE OR CHEF'S KNIFE

Onions need to be peeled by removing the skin and the first, tough outer layer. If onions are to be left whole, a knife should be used to slit and remove these layers. If they have been cut in half, the fingers can be used.

1. Using a chef's knife and the high technique, slice off the stem end.

2. Curl the last three fingers around the handle of the paring knife with the blade facing the fingertips. Place the index finger underneath the heel, close to the bolster. (It is possible to use the chef's knife to remove the peel. Grip the chef's knife in the same manner.)

3. Insert the heel of the blade under the skin, clamp the thumb over the skin, lift and rotate your wrist toward you, and pull the skin toward the root following the curve of the onion. Repeat this procedure to peel the entire onion and any tough outer layers.

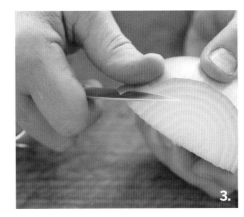

Rings

FRUIT OR VEGETABLE: ONIONS
KNIFE: 3½-INCH PARING KNIFE, CHEF'S KNIFE

Whole onion rings (usually red onions) are used in salads, but they can also be battered and deep-fried or grilled. For large Spanish or sweet onions, if you cannot complete the ring in one stroke, do not press straight down to finish the cut. Instead, use the high technique with the sawing motion as with cabbage (page 116).

1. Slice off the stem end with a chef's knife.

2. Peel using the paring knife or, if you feel bold enough, the chef's knife using the same grip and technique. It is sometimes useful to leave the skin bunched at the root end—it can make a useful handle as you work toward the root end.

3. Spread the fingers of your holding hand around the curve of the onion, using the knuckle of your middle finger as the stopper.

4. Use the high technique to cut rings to the desired thickness.

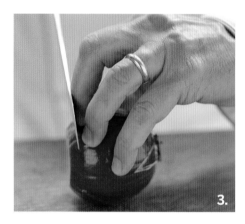

Half Rings

FRUIT OR VEGETABLE: ONIONS
KNIFE: CHEF'S KNIFE

1. Slice off the stem end.

2. Place stem-side down and cut in half through the middle of the root using the arc hold (page 85).

3. Peel each half with your fingers, a paring knife, or a chef's knife.

4. Place each half flat-side down on the board with the root facing your holding hand. Slice half-rings to the desired thickness.

Strips

FRUIT OR VEGETABLE: ONIONS
KNIFE: 3½-INCH PARING KNIFE, CHEF'S KNIFE

1. Slice off the stem and root ends with a chef's knife.

2. Cut in half lengthwise.

3. Peel each half with your fingers, a paring knife, or a chef's knife.

4. Place each half flat-side down on the board and cut into lengthwise strips.

Quarters or Chunks

FRUIT OR VEGETABLE: ONIONS
KNIFE: 3½-INCH PARING KNIFE, CHEF'S KNIFE

These will be perfectly fine for soups, stocks, and even some stews.

1. Slice off the stem and root ends with a chef's knife.

2. Cut in half lengthwise.

3. Peel each half with your fingers, a paring knife, or a chef's knife.

4. Place each half flat-side down on the board and cut in half for quarters. Cut quarters to the required size for chunks.

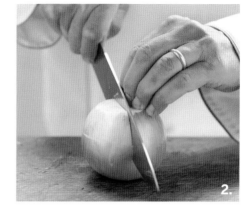

Dice

FRUIT OR VEGETABLE: ONIONS
KNIFE: 3½-INCH PARING KNIFE, CHEF'S KNIFE

Before you start cutting, determine the size of the final pieces because once they have been cut, they cannot be cut again. If you have made an uncorrectable error in cutting your first dice, get another onion and start again. While you can achieve the desired size, ⅛ inch to 1½ inches, by altering the number of parallel cuts, pulled cuts, and crosscuts you make, you will never get evenly sized pieces because the onion is concentrically layered, so the layers closer to the center have a smaller diameter. This is immutable— we just have to live with it.

Don't be daunted by all the steps that follow. Once you get the rhythm of the process, it will seem very logical and you'll be dicing onions like a pro.

1. Slice off the stem end with a chef's knife.

2. Place the onion stem-side down. Place the holding hand over half of the root end and cut through the middle of the root.

3. Peel each half with your fingers, a paring knife, or a chef's knife.

4. Place each half flat-side down at the near edge of the board, root facing your holding hand. Place the curved fingers of the holding hand firmly across the middle, making sure the thumb and pinky are not hanging over the sides as the knife is headed that way. Place the heel of the knife flush against the stem end, tip pointing straight ahead. Without cutting, pull the knife straight back three-quarters of the way. To start the cut, push forward and slightly toward the root end. Do not use any lateral force to move the knife toward the root end. Keep the tip pointed straight ahead.

5. Pull back in the groove just cut and repeat until you are close to the root. Stop and withdraw the knife. To make more than one parallel cut, start at the bottom of each half and work your way up.

6. Place the stem end at the near edge of the board, root facing away. Place the heel of the knife at the stem end, tip pointing up at about 45 degrees for a large onion, less of an angle for a smaller one.

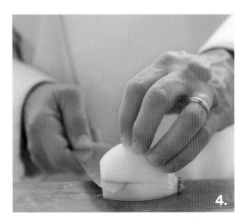

7. Maintaining this angle, pull the knife back and down through the onion until the tip is aligned with the root end.

8. Without stopping the motion, raise the handle to pull the tip from the root through and past the stem end, making sure you feel the tip on the board the whole time you are pulling. Follow through by pulling the tip of the knife off the board.

9. Reposition the blade and repeat this cut, making evenly spaced cuts across the whole onion.

10. The cuts can be perpendicular or radial (angling the knife at the sides to follow the onion's contour). Note that different lengths of the blade were used to make the pulls across the onion.

11. Return the onion to the horizontal position on the board and move it toward the far edge of the board by 2 or 3 inches.

12. Cut across the strips to get the desired dice.

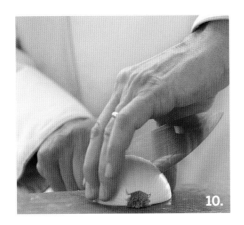

SHALLOTS

Shallots probably don't appear as often in your daily cooking as onions, but the same techniques are used to cut them, since they share the same concentrically layered structure. Unlike an onion, a shallot bulb often splits in half during growth. The split is covered by the skin and is not always apparent. After cutting off the stem end, pull the split halves apart, peel each half, and proceed as though you have cut the shallot in half.

Most often shallots are minced, but they can also be cut into rings, half rings, or strips. The chef's knife is too large and thick to deal with the smaller shallot. Depending on the size of the shallot, use a $3\frac{1}{2}$-inch paring knife or a 5- or 6-inch utility knife.

Since the $3\frac{1}{2}$-inch paring knife and 6-inch utility knife are small knives, I find it easier to use the high technique for removing the stem end and for doing the final crosscut. Try both the low and high techniques and decide which feels more comfortable. Frankly, it is quite difficult to use the low technique with a paring knife. Either way, remember to do your cutting close to the near edge of the board so you don't scrape your knuckles.

Mince

FRUIT OR VEGETABLE: SHALLOTS

KNIFE: 3½-INCH PARING KNIFE OR 5- OR 6-INCH UTILITY KNIFE

1. Slice off the stem end.

2. Place the shallot on its side and, using the arc hold (page 85), cut in half through the root making one or two angled cuts.

3. Peel each half with your fingers or a knife.

4. Place each half flat-side down at the near edge of the board and make one or two parallel cuts (page 87) using the fingers-closed (page 81) or fingers-bunched (page 83) hold.

5. Place the stem end at the near edge of the board, root facing away. Place the heel of the knife at the stem end, tip pointing up.

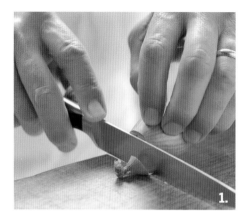

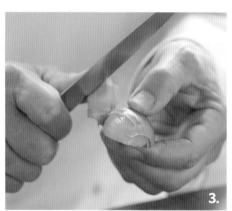

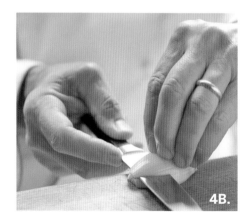

6. Maintaining this angle, pull the knife back and down through the shallot until the tip is aligned with the root end.

7. Without stopping the motion, raise the handle to pull the tip from the root through and past the stem end, making sure you feel the tip on the board the whole time you are pulling.Follow through by pulling the tip of the knife off the board. Place the knife in the pull position again and repeat, making close, evenly spaced cuts across the whole shallot.

8. Use the arc hold to make the pull near the holding hand.

9. Return the shallot to a horizontal position on the board. Using the high technique and either the fingers-closed (page 81) or fingers-bunched (page 83) hold, cut across the strips keeping the cuts very close together to get a mince.

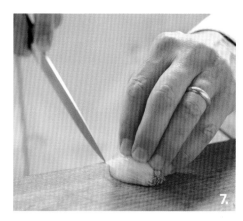

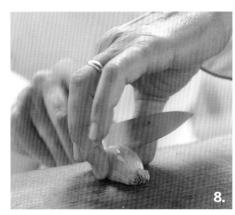

SCALLIONS

Dice or Mince

FRUIT OR VEGETABLE: SCALLION GREENS
KNIFE: CHEF'S KNIFE

Scallions, a member of the onion family, are often referred to as green onions, but they are milder in flavor than onions.

The white, root ends of the scallion are concentrically layered and tubular in shape. The hollow green stalks are usually removed and reserved for another use. I remove the top inch of green because that is where the sandy dirt hangs out.

1. Wash and dry the scallions. Bunch the scallions together and, using the last 3 or 4 inches of the chef's knife and the low technique, cut the green stalks into the size you need.

2. To mince the greens, pull the tip of the knife down the length of the greens. Bunch together and cut across to mince.

3. If using the whites, bunch as many as you need together and cut off the roots using the low technique.

4. Bunch together and cut crosswise to get the size you need using the low technique.

5. To mince, keep the root attached and pull the tip of the knife down the length one or two times.

6. Bunch together and cut across to mince.

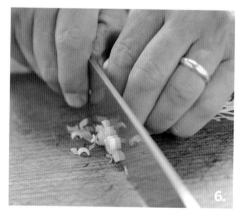

Shred

FRUIT OR VEGETABLE: SCALLIONS
KNIFE: CHEF'S KNIFE

These are generally used to garnish a Chinese main dish, and one always finds them on Cantonese-style steamed fish.

1. Cut off the top inch of the green portion and discard.

2. Place the greens vertically on the board and angle the knife to cut a 45-degree cross section, making cuts from top to bottom while maintaining the angle.

3. To shred the whites, cut off the roots, then remove the outer layer of the scallion with the fingers.

4. Place the whites vertically on the board and angle the knife to cut a 45-degree cross section, making the cuts from top to bottom while maintaining the angle.

CHIVES

Mince

FRUIT OR VEGETABLE: CHIVES
KNIFE: CHEF'S KNIFE

1. Trim the ends, bunch the chives together, and cut into a mince using the last 2 to 3 inches of the chef's knife and the low technique.

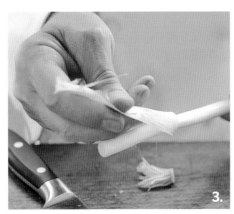

Cleaning Leeks

FRUIT OR VEGETABLE: LEEKS
KNIFE: CHEF'S KNIFE

The tubular pale green and white parts of the leek are what interest us. The dark green, tough leaves can be discarded or used to make a brown stock. The problem with leeks is the fine grains of sandy soil found at the base below where the leaves branch. There are several methods for cleaning leeks.

1. Slice off the tough green leaves about $^1\!/_2$ inch below the branch point but keep the root attached.

2. Then dig the point of the knife into the center of the leek nearest the root and pull it through to the other end.

3. Swish the leek in a bowl of cold water, spreading the layers apart with your fingers to rinse thoroughly.

Rings

FRUIT OR VEGETABLE: LEEKS
KNIFE: CHEF'S KNIFE

1. Cut the leek crosswise from the pale green section to the root end, to the desired thickness.

2. Place the slices in a bowl of cold water for several minutes. Drain and dry, if necessary.

Strips or Julienne

FRUIT OR VEGETABLE: LEEKS
KNIFE: CHEF'S KNIFE

1. Split the leek by digging the point of the knife lengthwise down the leek and pulling it out at the other end.

2. Place 4 or 5 layers flat-side down and vertically on the board. Cut strips to the desired thickness, using the low technique.

1.

2.

1A.

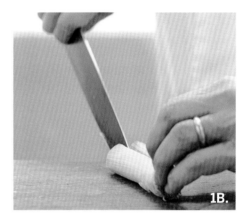

1B.

2A.

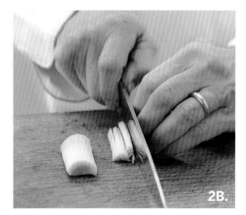

2B.

Rings

FRUIT OR VEGETABLE: BELL PEPPERS
KNIFE: CHEF'S KNIFE AND 6-INCH UTILITY KNIFE

1. Using the chef's knife, slice off the top of the pepper just below the stem, and the bottom about ½ inch from the end.

2. Insert the utility knife through the stem end and skim it along the inside curve of the pepper as you turn the pepper to the left (or right) to remove the membranes and seeds.

3. Place the pepper horizontally on the board and, with the chef's knife, cut the rings to the desired thickness using the high technique.

1.

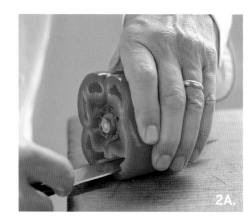
2A.

2B.

3.

Strips or Dice

FRUIT OR VEGETABLE: BELL PEPPERS
KNIFE: CHEF'S KNIFE OR 6-INCH UTILITY KNIFE

I first saw this technique demonstrated by my colleague and television personality Martin Yan. Be sure to buy straight peppers with three or four lobes—the twisted kind will not work.

The height of the pepper will determine whether a utility knife or a chef's knife should be used.

1. Slice off the top of the pepper just below the stem, and the bottom about $1/2$ inch from the end.

2. Angle the blade to the right (or left) and cut into a lobe crease.

3. Turn the blade toward your holding hand until it is parallel and skim it along the inside curve of the pepper as you pull the pepper open to the left (or right). You now have a flat pepper ready for slices, strips, or dice.

4. To remove the inner membrane, cut a 3- or 4-inch-wide strip of pepper. Place the strip horizontally on the board with the skin side down and, using the parallel position, zigzag the back half of the knife toward the left (or right) just under the spongy inside membrane, keeping the holding hand about $1/2$ inch ahead of the knife until the membrane is removed.

5. Cut the pepper into strips, then dice if desired.

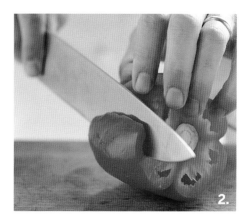

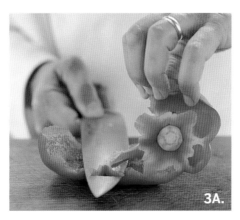

Seed and Dice

FRUIT OR VEGETABLE: CHILE PEPPERS
KNIFE: 6-INCH UTILITY KNIFE OR
  3½-INCH PARING KNIFE

The capsaicin kick in chile peppers comes primarily from the membranes that run the length of the pepper and to which the seeds are attached.

1. If I want the kick, I cut the pepper crosswise into wheels and leave the membrane and skin attached.

2. To remove the seeds, trim off the stem end and split the pepper in half lengthwise.

3. Use the tip of the paring knife to remove the membranes and seeds.

4. Cut the pepper into strips, then dice if desired.

Caution: Be sure to wash your hands thoroughly after handling chile peppers or, wear thin kitchen gloves.

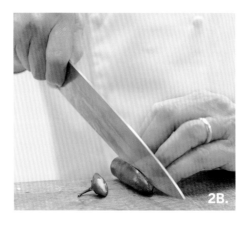

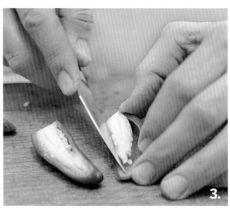

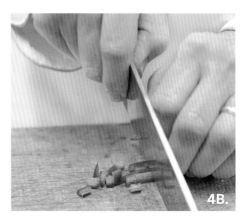

TOMATOES

Core

FRUIT OR VEGETABLE: TOMATOES
KNIFE: 3½-INCH PARING KNIFE

For coring grip see pages 108 and 109.

1. Hold the tomato stem-side up in the palm of the holding hand and angle it toward the knife hand. With an inch of knife showing above your thumb, insert the tip of the knife at a 45-degree angle, edge facing you, into the side of the core until your thumb makes contact with the tomato. Your thumb must stay in contact with the top of the core until it is removed.

2. Rotate the knife hand toward you until the knuckles are facing up. Hold the tomato firmly and rotate the knife hand back to the starting position (knuckles facing away) while simultaneously turning the tomato toward you. Three or four turns should remove the core.

1A.

1B.

2A.

2B.

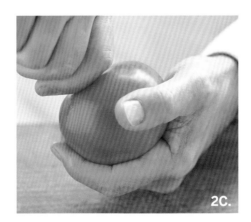

2C.

2D.

Peel

FRUIT OR VEGETABLE: TOMATOES
KNIFE: 3½-INCH PARING KNIFE

1. To peel a tomato, I usually core it first, then start the peeling from the blossom (bottom) end.

2. Cup the handle of the knife with four fingers with the blade in the parallel position.

3. Place the thumb on the near side of the tomato and make back-and-forth cuts until the top is nearly off.

4. Angle the tip of the blade up and to the right (or left) and, with the blade just under the skin, pivot the knife back and forth as you, rotate the tomato toward the knife with the holding hand until the peel is removed.

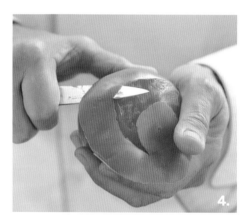

Dice

FRUIT OR VEGETABLE: TOMATOES
KNIFE: CHEF'S KNIFE

Core the tomato and cut a thin slice from top and bottom using the high technique.

1. Stand the tomato upright. Cut off the four "sides" following the curves. Remove any seeds with the fingers.

2. Cut the sides into strips the thickness of the desired dice.

3. Turn the strips horizontally and cut crosswise for the dice.

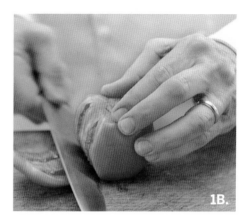

Concassé

FRUIT OR VEGETABLE: TOMATOES
KNIFE: CHEF'S KNIFE

Concassé is usually defined as a rough chop (but we don't chop, do we?). For some dishes the skin may be left on.

1. Core the tomato. Cut the tomato in half at its equator and squeeze to remove the seeds, but leave the fleshy center.

2. Give the tomatoes a rough cut using the high technique, turning them several times.

Slice

FRUIT OR VEGETABLE: TOMATOES
KNIFE: 10-INCH SCALLOPED-EDGE OR CHEF'S KNIFE

1. Core the tomato (see page 137). Place the tomato on the board, balanced on its equator, and slice to the desired thickness from the stem end to the blossom end using the high technique.

2. Use the parallel technique to get those last slices.

Wedge

FRUIT OR VEGETABLE: TOMATOES
KNIFE: CHEF'S KNIFE OR SCALLOPED-EDGE KNIFE

I recommend coring the tomato before cutting it into wedges. This will save you from having to cut the top from each wedge.

1. Cut the tomato in half from stem to blossom (top to bottom).

2. Place flat-side down and cut each half in half, then in half again for smaller wedges.

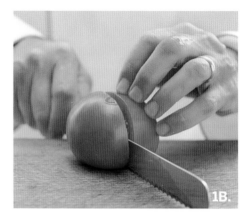

Separating Florets and Stalk

FRUIT OR VEGETABLE: BROCCOLI
KNIFE: CHEF'S KNIFE AND 6-INCH UTILITY KNIFE

You should treat broccoli as two separate vegetables—the florets and the stalks. The latter can be perfectly respectable if properly treated. Unless you want mushy florets, you cannot cook them while they are attached to the stalk. If you cook them until the stalks are done, the florets will only be suitable for the compost heap.

1. Cut the florets from the stalk at the point where they begin to branch. They will not yield evenly sized pieces.

2. Split the larger florets in half or thirds by cutting down the stem then tearing them apart by hand.

3. Remove the tough outer skin from the florets using the peeling grip. Remove the tough outer skin of the stalk by cutting down the sides. Alternately, insert the heel of the blade under the skin and rotate towards your holding hand.

4. To expose more surface area for quicker cooking, cut thin slices at a 45-degree angle, or cut the stalk across the middle.

5. To shred (for slaw) cut a two to three inch section crosswise and peel. Cut thin lengthwise slices using the high technique, then cut into shreds using the low technique.

Chop

FRUIT OR VEGETABLE: HERBS
KNIFE: CHEF'S KNIFE

You are finally going to get a chance to chop—the back end of the knife actually comes straight down on the leaves. Flat-leaf (Italian) parsley and cilantro may be chopped, as can rosemary needles. Wash and dry the leaves thoroughly, keeping them on the stems especially if you are using a spinner to dry them.

If you need only a small amount, ¼ cup or so, you can use the low technique to remove some of the leaves; otherwise remove the stems before chopping.

1. To chop, start with the basic chef's-knife grip, then let go with the ring and pinky fingers. Hold the tip of the knife down with the palm of the holding hand.

2. Pivot on the tip to the far side and, as you do so, slap or bounce the back half of the knife straight down with your wrist. The tip stays anchored to the board by your palm the whole time. Pivot and bounce (chop) as you move to the far side of the bunched leaves. Keep the cuts very close together.

3. At the far end, lower the back end of the knife and scoop the leaves back into a small pile. Repeat the process of chopping and gathering until you have the desired size, either coarsely or finely chopped (minced).

Chiffonade

FRUIT OR VEGETABLE: BASIL
KNIFE: CHEF'S KNIFE

Unlike parsley, basil cannot be chopped because chopping will bruise the leaves and they will turn brown. The chiffonade cut uses a gliding motion of the knife to finely shred the leaves.

1. Stack several leaves and roll them into a cylinder.

2. Using the low technique, glide the knife through with a forward push to cut into thin ribbons.

GARLIC

Garlic can be used whole, sliced, minced, or mashed either through a press or with the spine of a paring knife. Unless it is being roasted, garlic should always be peeled.

Mince

FRUIT OR VEGETABLE: GARLIC
KNIFE: 3½-INCH PARING KNIFE OR CHEF'S KNIFE

1. Cut off the root end at the heel of the chef's knife (low technique) Gently tap the clove with the flat of the blade to split the skin. Remove the skin.

2. Cut a peeled clove in half lengthwise.

3. Place the halves horizontally at the front edge of the board with the root facing your holding hand. Make one or two parallel cuts.

4. Place the clove vertically on the board, root facing away. Place the heel of the knife at the front end, tip pointing up and make pulled cuts all the way across, as you did with onions and shallots.

5. Turn the clove horizontally and use the high technique to cut across into a mince.

Alternately, peeled cloves can be crushed with the flat of the chef's knife by giving a hard tap, coming off the knife immediately after contact. Proceed to chop as for parsley.

1A.

1B.

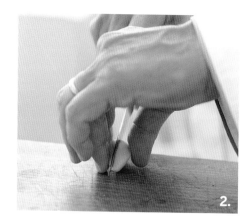

2.

3.

4.

5.

Slice

FRUIT OR VEGETABLE: GARLIC
KNIFE: CHEF'S KNIFE

1. Using the low technique, cut a peeled clove into slices. To do this with a paring knife is far too tedious. You could use a utility knife, but using a chef's knife is less work.

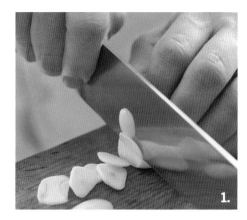

Puree

FRUIT OR VEGETABLE: GARLIC
KNIFE: 3½-INCH PARING KNIFE

Occasionally you'll need a teaspoon or so of garlic puree.

1. Cut a large clove of peeled garlic in half lengthwise.

2. Place each half flat-side down at the near edge of the board. Place your index finger on the heel of the blade and angle the blade up, spine on the garlic.

3. Scrape across the top of the clove getting a good follow-through.

Peeled

FRUIT OR VEGETABLE: GINGER
KNIFE: 3½-INCH PARING KNIFE

If the ginger is fresh with a tight, pale skin, it can be peeled with the spine of the knife.

1. With the thumb of the knife hand at the top of the ginger for support, use the spine of the blade to scrape from bottom to top all around.

Mince

FRUIT OR VEGETABLE: GINGER
KNIFE: CHEF'S KNIFE

Many Chinese recipes call for minced ginger, and they don't mean grated ginger. The process is the same as for finely dicing a solid item, but since ginger is very fibrous, be sure to cut thin lengthwise slices following the lengthwise grain. Thick pieces are not easy to chew.

1. Using the high technique, cut very thin slices of peeled ginger, following the grain.

2. Stack several slices and cut into shreds thinner than matchsticks, again with the grain.

3. Turn the shreds and cut across to mince.

STRAWBERRIES

Hull

FRUIT OR VEGETABLE: STRAWBERRIES
KNIFE: 3½-INCH PARING KNIFE

Hulling strawberries is done in the same manner as coring a tomato but less of the knife's tip is used.

1. Remove the green calyx with your fingers.

2. Hold the strawberry hull-side up in the palm of your holding hand and angle it toward your knife hand.

3. Insert the tip of the knife at a 45-degree angle, edge facing you, into the side of the white core until your thumb makes contact with the strawberry. Your thumb should stay in contact with the strawberry until the core is removed.

4. Rotate the knife hand toward you until your knuckles are facing up. Rotate the knife hand back to the starting position (knuckles facing away) while turning the strawberry toward you. Two or three turns should remove the hull.

Quarter or Slice

FRUIT OR VEGETABLE: STRAWBERRIES
KNIFE: CHEF'S KNIFE, 6-INCH UTILITY KNIFE, OR 3½-INCH PARING KNIFE

1. If you don't care how the cut pieces fall, hull the strawberry and use the utility or chef's knife to cut halves or quarters. You may even use the pairing knife and the snippy grip (page 106).

2. If you want thin slices cut through but kept in slice order, hull the strawberry. Place vertically on the board. Use the arc hold and place the tip of the utility knife on the board and raise the handle to form a 45-degree angle. Keeping the angle, pull the knife through the strawberry. Repeat until completely sliced.

3. Press down to fan out the slices.

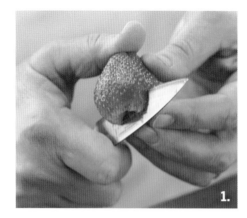

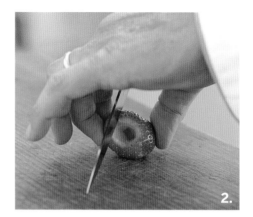

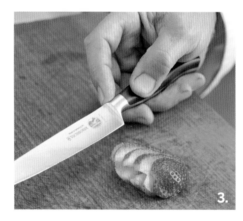

Peel and Core

FRUIT OR VEGETABLE: APPLES
KNIFE: 3½-INCH PARING KNIFE OR
   6-INCH UTILITY KNIFE,

Use these techniques to prepare
apples for pies, tarts, or fruit salads.
Most recipes will call for cored,
peeled apples.

1. Remove the core with an apple corer.

2. Cut a thin slice from top and bottom.
   Then with the back third of a utility
   knife or with a paring knife, peel
   using the peeling grip for round fruits
   (page 105).

Wedge

FRUIT OR VEGETABLE: APPLES
KNIFE: 6-INCH UTILITY KNIFE OR CHEF'S KNIFE

1. Cut the cored apple in half lengthwise.

2. To cut the apple into eight wedges,
   place the flat sides down and cut each
   half in half, then in half again.

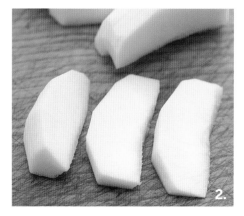

Thin Slices

FRUIT OR VEGETABLE: APPLES
KNIFE: 6-INCH UTILITY KNIFE

1. Trim ¼ to ½ inch from the top and bottom of the cored apple, making the cuts as parallel as possible, then peel.

2. Cut the cored apple in half lengthwise. Place the halves flat-side down, place the tip of the knife on the board, and raise the handle to form a 45-degree angle. Pull the knife toward you and through the apple, using the guide hand to achieve the desired thickness.

3. At first this will seem slow but speed will come with practice. When you are finished slicing, press the slices with your hand so they fan out. The slices can then be picked up in one layer and placed on the tart dough or wherever you want them.

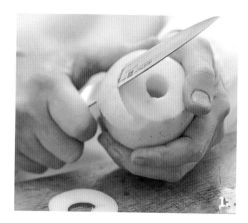

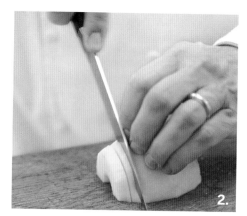

Dice

FRUIT OR VEGETABLE: APPLES
KNIFE: 6-INCH UTILITY KNIFE OR CHEF'S KNIFE

1. Core the apple, peeled or unpeeled.

2. Determine the size dice you will need and cut the appropriate number of wedges.

3. Trim the wedges to size if necessary, then cut across to dice.

Rings

FRUIT OR VEGETABLE: PINEAPPLES
KNIFE: 10-INCH SCALLOPED EDGE AND UTILITY KNIFE

Pineapple is always peeled before being cut into rings or pieces.

1. To peel, trim off about 1 inch from the top and bottom.

2. Stand the pineapple on one end and work the knife down and around the sides, removing enough of the outer flesh so that no eyes are visible.

3. Cut the peeled pineapple in half crosswise.

4. Remove the tough inner core with the utility knife, following the outlines of the core.

5. Cut each half into rings.

6. Cut the last rings using a zigzag, parallel motion.

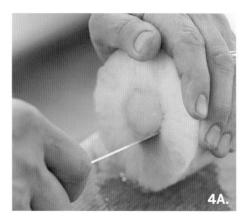

Pieces

FRUIT OR VEGETABLE: PINEAPPLES
KNIFE: 10-INCH SCALLOPED-EDGE KNIFE AND 6-INCH UTILITY KNIFE, OR CHEF'S KNIFE

1. Slice off the top and bottom of the pineapple using the scalloped-edge knife and the high technique.

2. Turn the pineapple vertically and use the same knife and technique to cut in half, then in half again.

3. Place each wedge horizontally on the board. With the knife in parallel position set the heel just underneath the core. Pull towards you and zig-zag towards your holding hand. The push resets the blade for the next pull. Discard the core.

4. Use this same starting point and technique to remove the skin.

5. To slice, place each wedge horizontally on the board. Place the tip of the utility knife on the board and raise the handle to form a 45-degree angle. Pull toward you and through to separate. Continue all the way across.

6. For smaller pieces place each quarter vertically. Pull through, turn horizontally. Pull through to cut the pieces.

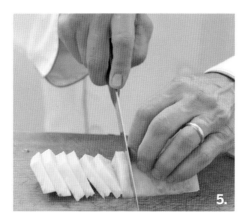

Slices and Pieces

FRUIT OR VEGETABLE: MANGO
KNIFE: 6-INCH UTILITY KNIFE

The mango is oval with an oval-shaped, somewhat flat seed in the middle.

1. Cut a thin slice from the bottom.

2. Stand the mango upright. Remove each side by cutting forward and down to the left and right of the center seed.

3. For large slices, use the peeling grip and a back-and-forth motion to peel each half.

4. Place the peeled halves flat-side down horizontally on the board. Place the tip of the knife on the board and raise the handle to form a 45-degree angle. Pull the knife toward you and through. Reset the blade and use the holding hand to achieve the desired thickness.

5. For smaller slices or pieces, place each unpeeled half vertically on the board and cut in half lengthwise.

6. Place each quarter horizontally on the board. With the knife in parallel position, place the heel between flesh and skin. Pull the knife toward you and use the parallel, zigzag technique following the mango's contour. The push resets the blade for the next pull.

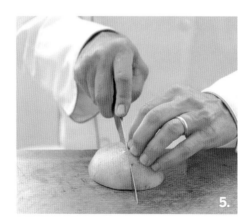

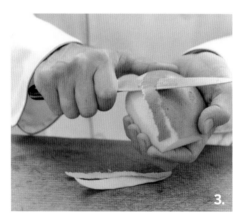

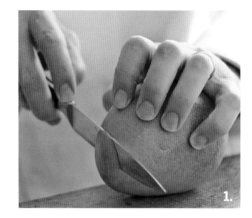

7. To slice, use the chef's knife and the low technique.

8. Alternately use the pull through technique of step 4 with the utility knife.

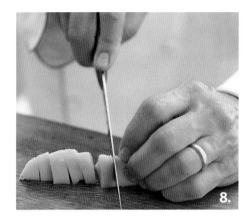

Cubes

FRUIT OR VEGETABLE: MANGO

KNIFE: 6-INCH UTILITY KNIFE OR 3½-INCH PARING KNIFE

1. Place a mango half skin-side down on the board or hold it in your hand and carefully crosshatch diagonally across the flesh.

2. Turn the mango half inside out and scrape the cubes from the skin.

Suprême

FRUIT OR VEGETABLE: ORANGES
KNIFE: 6-INCH UTILITY KNIFE

1. Cup the handle of the knife with four fingers. Hold the orange in the holding hand, with the thumb on the peel, thumbnail facing you. Place the knife against the peel and move the knife back and forth, cutting in both directions. Keep the knife edge angled slightly up, just underneath the peel, so you don't cut into the orange's flesh. As you cut, turn the orange toward the knife with the holding hand and move the knife lower with each turn, to remove a long spiral of peel.

2. Once the peel is removed, trim away any remaining white membrane.

3. Hold the peeled orange over a bowl and remove the segments by cutting just to the left of a membrane, following the curve of the orange front and back all the way to the center. Do the same on the right side of the segment and flick the membrane-free orange segments into the bowl.

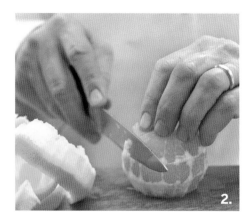

Wedges

FRUIT OR VEGETABLE: ORANGES

KNIFE: 6-INCH UTILITY KNIFE OR 10-INCH
    SCALLOPED-EDGE KNIFE

Almost every Chinese meal in an
American Chinatown restaurant ends
with orange wedges. Be prepared to
pick up a wedge, bend back the ends,
and work the flesh from the peel with
your teeth.

1. Cut the orange in half at the equator,
   not from pole to pole.

2. Lay the halves cut-side down. Cut
   them in half, then in half again.

Suprême

FRUIT OR VEGETABLE: GRAPEFRUITS

KNIFE: 8- OR 10-INCH SERRATED KNIFE OR 6-INCH
   UTILITY KNIFE

1. Tip the grapefruit on its side and remove the top and bottom using two or three angled, forward strokes.

2. Set the grapefruit up on one of its flat ends and use three or four forward and downward strokes to remove as much pitch with the peel and as little of the flesh as possible, working the knife down the sides to follow the curve of the fruit. Once the peel is removed, trim away any remaining white membrane.

3. Hold the peeled grapefruit over a bowl and remove the segments by cutting just to the left of a membrane, following the curve of the segment front and back all the way to the center. Do the same on the right side of the segment and flick the membrane-free grapefruit segments into the bowl.

1.

2A.

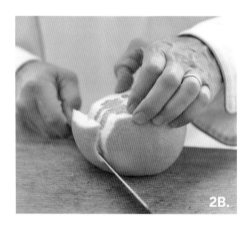

2B.

3A.

3B.

Wedges

FRUIT OR VEGETABLE: GRAPEFRUITS
KNIFE: 8- OR 10-INCH SCALLOPED-EDGE KNIFE

1. Cut the grapefruit in half at the equator not from pole to pole. If this cannot be accomplished in one stroke, pull the knife back in the groove just cut and make another forward, angled cut.

2. Lay the halves cut side down. Cut each in half, then in half again using the high technique.

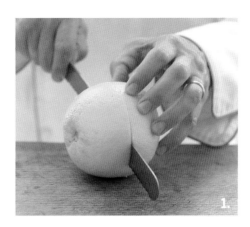

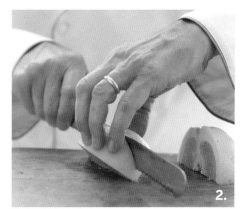

LEMONS AND LIMES

Wedges

FRUIT OR VEGETABLE: LEMONS AND LIMES

KNIFE: 6-INCH UTILITY KNIFE OR 5-INCH TOMATO
KNIFE

1. Trim both ends of the fruit.
   Cut in half lengthwise.

2. Cut into equally sized wedges.
   Cut the wedges in half crosswise
   for squeezable pieces.

Slices

FRUIT OR VEGETABLE: LEMONS AND LIMES

KNIFE: 6-INCH UTILITY KNIFE OR
5-INCH TOMATO KNIFE

1. To get slices of citrus that rest
   beautifully on the rim of a glass, trim
   both ends of the fruit. Make a $1/2$-inch
   lengthwise cut.

2. Turn the fruit horizontally and cut $1/4$-
   inch slices, or thinner.

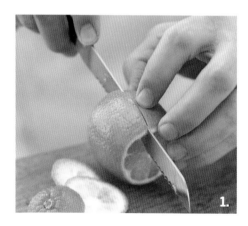

Wedges

FRUIT OR VEGETABLE: CANTALOUPE
KNIFE: 10-INCH SCALLOPED-EDGE KNIFE
  OR CHEF'S KNIFE

If the melon has clearly defined and equally distributed segments such as on some cantaloupe or Persian varieties, you may use those as markers. If you want smaller or larger wedges, or if the melon has no pronounced segments,

1. Cut the melon in half from top to bottom using the high technique.

2. Remove the seeds with a tablespoon. Place flat-side down and cut in half using the high technique.

3. For quarters, cut in half again using the arc hold and the high technique.

Pieces

FRUIT OR VEGETABLE: CANTALOUPE
KNIFE: 6-INCH UTILITY KNIFE

1. Place a melon wedge horizontally on the board, skin-side down. Place the heel of the utility knife on the right (or left) side and pull toward the holding hand to cut, keeping the knife in contact with the skin and following the melon's contour. The push resets the blade for the next pull.

2. To cut the melon into pieces, place the tip of the knife on the board and raise the handle to form a 45-degree angle above the peeled melon slice.

3. Pull the knife toward you and through the melon, using the holding hand to achieve the desired thickness.

1.

2.

3.

PLUMS, PEACHES, AND NECTARINES

Slices

FRUIT OR VEGETABLE: PLUMS, PEACHES, AND
NECTARINES
KNIFE: 6-INCH UTILITY KNIFE

All of these fruits have a center pit and a crease near the stem end.

1. Place the edge of the knife in the crease of the fruit and make a cut toward the pit.

2. Keeping the knife straight and in the crease, pull it from top to bottom while rotating the fruit away from the knife hand.

3. Use a spoon or your fingers to remove the pit.

4. Place the halves flat-side down, place the tip of the knife on the board, and raise the handle to form a 45-degree angle. Pull the knife toward you and through the fruit, using the guide hand to achieve the desired thickness.

DECORATIVE GARNISHES

A decorative garnish is designed to call attention to itself and to add beauty to the dish it is garnishing. Here are a few of my favorites, none of which requires any special tools.

Strawberry Fans

FRUIT OR VEGETABLE: STRAWBERRIES
KNIFE: 3½-INCH PARING KNIFE OR 6-INCH UTILITY KNIFE

Fanning is accomplished by pulling the knife toward you as you cut thin, angled segments while keeping the back of the stem attached. Large strawberries are often cut in half before fanning; smaller ones may be fanned whole.

1. Cut the strawberry in half lengthwise and leave the green calyx attached Place the heel of the knife at the tip of the strawberry, angled up at about 25 degrees. Pull the knife through as you did for the onion (page 126).

2. Use the whole blade to make evenly spaced and perpendicular cuts all the way across.

3. When all the cuts are completed, press down with the knife or your hand to create the fan.

Lemon Stars

FRUIT OR VEGETABLE: LEMONS
KNIFE: 3½-INCH PARING KNIFE

1. Trim a thin slice from each end of the lemon. Pick any spot in the center of the lemon and, using the paring knife, make 25- to 45-degree angle cuts through the rind to the center all around the circumference, the last cut meeting the first.

2. Twist the lemon apart to make two stars.

Orange Basket

FRUIT OR VEGETABLE: ORANGES
KNIFE: 6-INCH UTILITY KNIFE

In addition to the knife, you will also need a 6- or 8-inch bamboo skewer unless you have a good eye. This technique can also be used for melons.

1. Trim a thin slice off the bottom of the orange so that the basket will sit flat. Insert a skewer horizontally through the center of the orange.

2. Form the handle by cutting downward ¼ to ⅜ inch on either side of center to the skewer.

3. Make horizontal cuts in line with the skewer on each side to meet the handle cuts.

4. Remove the flesh between the handle and the cup.

5. Notch the edges of the cup all the way around.

1.

2.

3.

3A.

4A.

4B.

5.

Tomato Roses

FRUIT OR VEGETABLE: TOMATOES
KNIFE: 3½-INCH PARING KNIFE

1. Core the tomato.

2. Almost slice off the flower end but before completing the cut tilt the knife upward to begin peeling the skin in one continuous thin strip, using a back-and-forth motion with the knife. Turn the tomato towards the moving knife.

3. Curl the strip tightly, skin-side out, taking care not to twist it.

4. Place the base (flower end) on top. Turn it over—and voilà!

Cucumber Flying Fish

FRUIT OR VEGETABLE: CUCUMBER
KNIFE: 6-INCH UTILITY KNIFE OR
3½-INCH PARING KNIFE

Use a seedless cucumber for this garnish.

1. Slice off about 1 inch from one end. Cut the cucumber into 3½- to 4-inch sections, then cut in half lengthwise

2. Cut off the right (or left) end at a 45-degree angle.

3. Now make 7 cuts: numbers 1, 3, and 5 each about ⅛-inch thick, pulling the knife as for the strawberry fan, and keeping the back attached; numbers 2, 4, and 6 should be as thin as possible. (Be sure to follow the 45-degree angle for each cut; number 7 separates the other cuts from the rest of the cucumber.)

4. Fold cut 2 back to 1, cut 4 back to 3, cut 6 back to 5.

3A.

1.

3B.

2.

4.

CHAPTER NINE

Fabricating Poultry, Meat, and Fish

DISJOINTING A CHICKEN AND BONING THE BREAST

For the task of chicken fabrication, I prefer to use a very sharp, rigid, 5-inch boning knife, although I have done it with cleavers and even that 8-inch chef's knife. Learning the technique means you don't have to pay a butcher. In addition, if you make your own stocks and soups, the backs, necks, and all the bones are yours for the taking.

You basically want to keep the knife in the same starting position for many of the cuts, turning the chicken to accommodate your arm and your knife. All but one of the cuts are made by pulling the knife toward you. Sometimes one cut will do; other times you will need to make overlapping pulls. Avoid moving the knife in a back-and-forth motion.

The bones are your guideposts, so before you attempt this task, use your eyes and fingers to familiarize yourself with the anatomy of the bird. The goal in fabrication is to cut through skin to expose the joints, then to separate the bones at these joints rather than to try to cut through the bone. The only bones that need cutting are the thin rib bones and the breastbone if you want to split it.

Removing
the Wings

KNIFE: 5-INCH BONING KNIFE

1. Place the chicken breast-side down on the board with the tail angled toward your knife-hand hip. Use your index finger to locate the end of the wing bone. The object is to separate the wing taking along as little breast meat as possible.

2. Hold on to the last joint. Place the heel of the blade almost flat against the neck at the wing joint (in the armpit). Pull to expose the joint. Snap the wing back to separate the shoulder bone from the socket. Make a circular cut behind the wing joint away from the breast and cut through the ligaments to separate. The knife should end up on the cutting board.

3. Turn the chicken around so that the other wing and your knife are in the same position as for the first wing and remove.

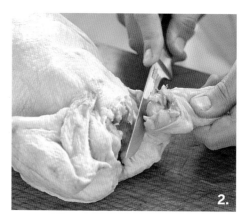

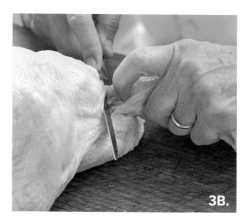

Removing Leg and Thigh

KNIFE: 5-INCH BONING KNIFE

1. Turn the chicken breast-side up with the tail angled toward your knife-hand hip. Cut through the flap of skin between the leg and thigh following the contour of the thigh. Pull toward the tail, keeping the knife almost parallel to the body.

2. Run your fingers down the thigh until you feel the end of the bone. Use upward pressure with the fingers to snap the bone out of the hip socket.

3. Using the lower backbone as a guide, start at the tail and make overlapping pulls toward then through the thigh. Turn the chicken around and remove the other leg and thigh.

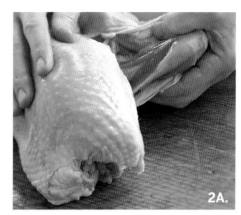

Removing the Lower Back

KNIFE: 5-INCH BONING KNIFE

1. Place the chicken on its side with the tail angled toward your knife-hand hip. Note the two flaps of thin connective tissue below the lower breast.

2. Plunge the tip of the knife through top and bottom flaps, then lower the knife and pull to sever both flaps in one cut.

3. Grasp the lower back with the hand and snap up toward the head to separate at the coccyx. I refer to the technique as "plunge, lower, pull."

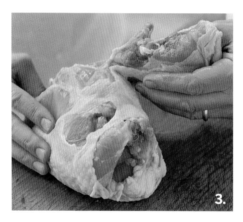

Removing the Upper Back and Neck

KNIFE: 5-INCH BONING KNIFE

1. Place the chicken on its side with the tail angled toward your knife-hand hip. Pull the upper portion of the skin back to expose the line of fat that appears next to the skin in the middle of the rib cage.

2. Keep the knife parallel to the fat and plunge the tip of the knife to the board.

3. Lower the heel to cut the top ribs. Pull toward your knife-hand hip to cut the lower ribs.

4. Grasp the neck and lower rib bones. Snap the back straight toward the head and break as you would a bunch of sticks. A little pulling might be necessary to separate the back from the shoulder ligaments.

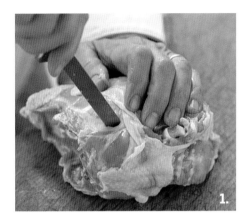

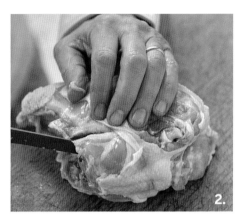

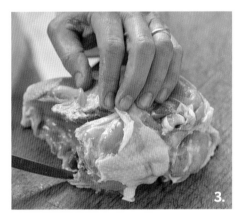

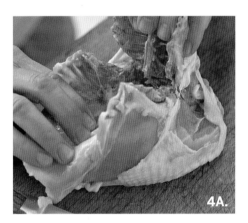

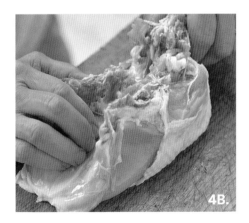

Boning the Breast from the Back

KNIFE: 5-INCH BONING KNIFE

1. Place the chicken skin-side down on the board, with the tail angled toward your knife-hand hip. Locate the white piece of collagen at the top of the breastbone.

2. Push the knife to cut the collagen through the center while holding the knife at a 45-degree angle. Stop when you reach the top of the breastbone.

3. Lightly pull the tip of the knife down the breastbone to split the membrane that covers it.

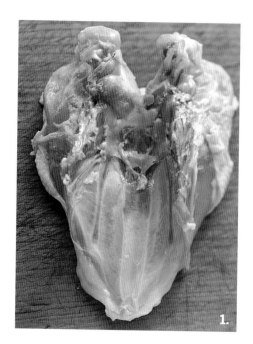

4. Pick up the chicken with both hands. Starting on either side, place your holding-hand thumb on the breastbone and your other thumb on the split collagen, your fingers underneath the breast.

5. Snap upward in the center and downward at the side of the breast to expose one side of the breastbone. Repeat this on the other side.

6. Work your fingers along the bone from head to tail to remove it from its sheath.

7. Holding the top of the breast down, grasp the top of the bone and pull it upward and toward the tail to remove it.

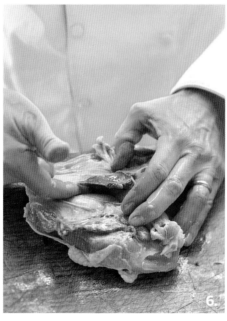

Getting It Boneless

KNIFE: 5-INCH BONING KNIFE

To get a boneless breast, remove the ribs and whatever bones remain in the shoulder area.

1. Place the tip of the knife underneath one side of the split collagen. I start on the left side.

2. Using overlapping, pulling strokes, work the tip downward along the ribs toward the long, thin bone near the bottom of the breast.

3. When this bone is loosened, grasp it at the end and, using the tip of the knife, scrape upwards along the ribs toward the shoulder using short, overlapping strokes.

4. Grasp the bones and snap backward to remove. A little pulling or twisting might be necessary. You will have to turn your arm outward to do the other side.

5. Very often the wishbone breaks during the above process. Pull out whatever is pullable. Use the tip of the boning knife to carefully scrape away the meat from the half that remains.

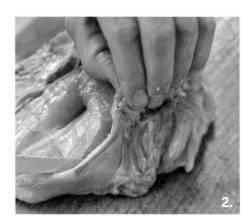

Separating the Leg and Thigh

KNIFE: 5-INCH BONING KNIFE

You now have your basic parts. Here's how to fabricate the smaller pieces.

1. Place the leg and thigh on the board with the skin side down.

2. Use your index finger to locate the space between the two bones. With the knife against the finger, pull to separate. Usually there is a distinct line of fat right over the joint. Place the heel of your knife just to the left of the line of fat and pull to separate.

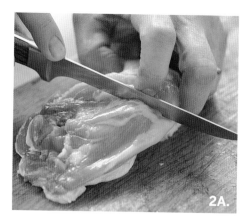

Splitting a Bone-In Breast

1. Use a heavy knife for this job (a 10-inch chef's knife will do). Under no circumstances should you try to use a chopping technique with anything but a serious cleaver. Your chef's knife edge is too delicate for chopping bones but can do the job if you place the edge right on the center of the bone.

2. Lift your hand and give the spine of the blade a whack with your open palm, thinking follow-through. As soon as your palm makes contact, lift it (think of clapping). Once split in half lengthwise, the breast can be quartered using the same method.

3. With the leg and thigh separated and the breast quartered, you now have eight neat portions. Add the wings (I'm partial to them) and you have ten pieces.

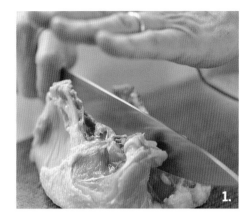

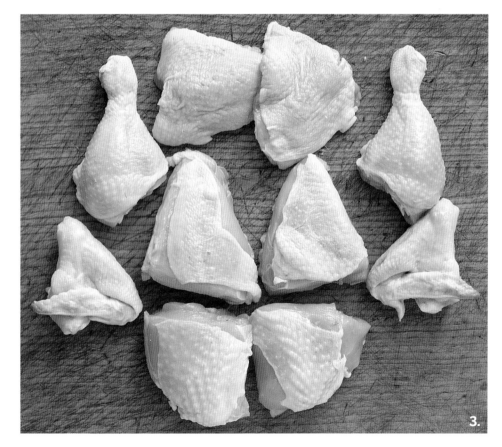

Removing the Skin and the Tenders

KNIFE: 5-INCH BONING KNIFE

The most expensive cut in the poultry section of the butcher shop is the cutlet. I have seen whole chickens sell for 79 or 89 cents per pound while the cutlet is selling for $4.99 or more. This is really where your boning knife pays for itself—quickly.

1. Once the breast has been boned out from the back and the skin has been removed, use your fingers to extract the tender finger, that delicate muscle that is encased in the center on the bone side of the breast. Sometimes it pulls out easily, sometimes it does not.

2. To facilitate removal, use your fingers to loosen the surrounding sheath as you gently pull the tender from top to bottom.

3. To remove the tendon, that whitish, chewy thing embedded in the center, place the tender rounded-side up at the edge of the cutting board. Grab the exposed tendon with your thumb and index finger. If it is too slippery, use a paper towel.

4. Holding it down with the spine of the boning knife, scrape away from you, while pulling the tendon toward you at the same time.

Now your chicken breast is boneless, skinless, and tendonless and ready for greater things.

Butterflying the Breast and Cutlets

KNIFE: 9-INCH GRANTON-EDGE CARVER

The breast should be butterflied from the outside toward the center. One is done skin-side up, the other skin-side down, working from the middle.

1. With the breast bone-side up, cut away the material in the middle that housed the breastbone so you have two halves. Trim any fat.

2. With your hand on top, use a 9- or 10-inch carving knife to make overlapping pulls in the parallel position from the top toward the center to the bottom. Don't try this in one motion. Reset the knife several times if necessary.

3. When close to the center, open the breast, lay it flat, and use delicate pulling strokes to even it out. The butterflied breast can now be stuffed and rolled.For chicken cutlets, cut the butterflied breast in half lengthwise and place bone-side up.

4. Wrap the breast in parchment paper or plastic wrap skin-side down and use a wooden mallet or stainless steel meat pounder to make the cutlet even from top to bottom. For the mallet use a delicate hammer like motion; for the pounder, use glancing blows away from you. Since the top half is thicker, that's the part you want to thin.

Boning the Breast From the Front

KNIFE: 5-INCH BONING KNIFE

I use this technique to remove the breast halves from a roasted chicken. They are then cut into crosswise portions and placed back in their original shape on the platter.

Use your fingers to locate the center of the backbone. With this as a guide,

1. Place the chicken skin-side up on the board with the tail facing away from you.

2. Run the knife along the outside of the bone from the bottom to the top of the breast, pulling the meat aside as you go. When you hit the wishbone follow it to the wing area.

3. Return the knife to the tail section and gently scrape the breast meat from the ribs. You can pull the meat away from the bones at this point.

4. Remove the second half in the same manner.

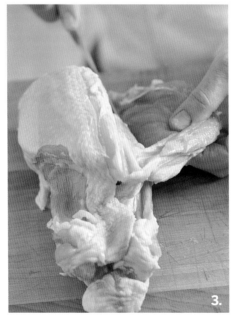

Boning the Thighs

KNIFE: 5-INCH BONING KNIFE

I prefer to use boneless thighs, usually diced, for Chinese cooking.

1. After removing the skin, place the thigh skin-side down with the top of the bone away from you.

2. Run the tip of the knife down each side of the bone to loosen the meat then insert the tip underneath, near the top to free it.

3. Hold the top of the bone and run the knife underneath it to the bottom. Remove bone and any surrounding gristle.

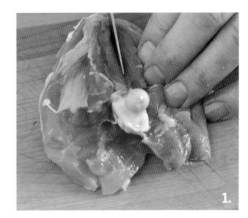

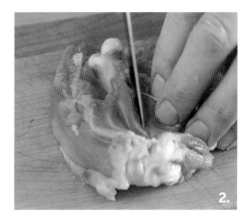

BUTTERFLYING A CENTER-CUT LOIN OF PORK

The whole loin of pork actually extends from the shoulder to the ham and is generally divided into three sections—the rib end, center cut, and loin end. We will be dealing with the center cut, the most uniform part of the loin but also the most difficult to cook because it has the least amount of fat. It's the "other white meat" and must not be overcooked. As a matter of fact, it should be tinged pink in the center when done. I don't take it above 150°F on the meat thermometer. By the time the carry-over cooking has taken place (the final rise in temperature that occurs as the roast rests), it reaches 155°F. Trichinosis, a parasite, is killed at 139°F to 140°F.

To roast any section of the loin whole, leave it on the bone. It can be removed from the bone after cooking using the technique on page 196. If you want to cook it on the bone but serve it as a chop, have the butcher remove the chine (backbone) and the attached feather bones for easy carving, and remove the parchmentlike film on the underside of the bones. In the picture at left, my index and middle finger are on the chine.

Boning and Butterflying a Center-Cut Loin of Pork

For a boneless roast, use a 5- or 6-inch boning knife to remove the meat from the ribs. A six-rib section is shown here.

1. Keep the knife against the ribs and follow the curvature, pulling the meat away as you go. Don't throw the bones away—roast them in the pan along with the meat. They make for good nibbling and a great sauce.

2. To butterfly the center cut, remove the flap of meat and fat that covered the bones. Don't throw this away either—trimmed, it makes great chili.

3. Place the roast fat-side down and make a pulled cut to the center.

4. Turn the knife sideways and cut toward the left end (right end if you're left-handed), stopping about an inch from the end, then use delicate pulling strokes to flatten the left side (right side) of the open book. Turn the roast around and do the other side.

5. The butterflied cut is now ready for stuffing, tying, and roasting.

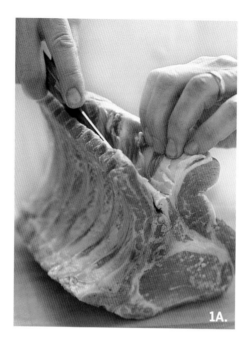
1A.

1B.

1C.

1D.

FRENCHING A RACK OF LAMB

A rack of lamb is delicious and expensive—costing between $15 and $18 per pound. The butcher will french it for you by scraping all meat and fat from the bones, but it is not that difficult to do yourself. Have the butcher remove the chine (backbone) identified in the photo on page 198. You will feel a great sense of pride and accomplishment bringing your handiwork to the table.

Lamb has a parchmentlike layer (the fell) that covers the fat and must be removed, unless the butcher has already removed it. In addition you will want to remove some of the fat. If I am going to roast the rack with a crumb mixture on top, I remove almost all the fat; otherwise I leave some on.

Frenching a Rack of Lamb

KNIFE: 5-INCH BONING KNIFE

1. To remove some of the fat, insert the tip of the boning knife under the fat and push it through about 2 or 3 inches. Make parallel cuts to the opposite side with slight upward pressure, keeping the knife against the layer of fat.

2. Make a pulled cut across the flap that covers the bones. Cut down to the bone then make overlapping, pulled cuts to the ends, pulling the flap away as you go.

3. Make a small incision between the feather bones to facilitate carving later.

4. Remove the membrane by inserting your finger or the end of a spoon under one side to loosen it, then pull it off.

5. Trim the fat on top of the exposed bones.

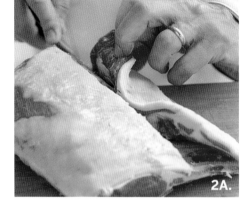

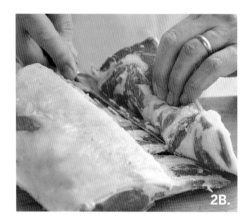

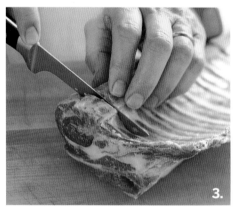

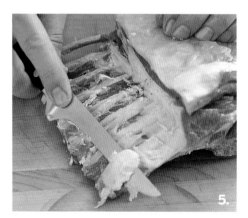

6. Remove as much material as you can from between the bones, then use the blade's edge to scrape until the bones are clean.

Preparing a Bias Cut Slice

Many Chinese dishes require bias-sliced meat, chicken, or fish. A flank steak is used here for demonstration purposes.

A 10-inch carving knife will produce a thin slice with one forward-and-back motion.

1. Place the steak on the board and make a long, pulled stroke toward you to cut the steak lengthwise to the desired width.

2. Position the strip horizontally at the near edge of the board. Place the knife where you want to start the cut. Raise the spine of the blade about $1/8$ inch. Place your fingers on top of the slice you are about to cut, using the fingers-closed position (page 81). Push the knife forward until the tip reaches the board. You will have cut more than halfway through at this point.

3. Pull the knife toward you until the slice is separated. In photo 3B one slice has already been removed to show the angle of the cut. Reposition the knife and repeat the push-pull cut, which is easily accomplished if you don't press down.

Cutting Stew Meat

KNIFE: 10-INCH CHEF'S KNIFE

Cutting a chuck or top or bottom round roast into cubes is similar to preparing a flank steak, at least for the first cut.

1. Place the meat on the board vertically. Cut into even strips using lengthwise pulls with the tip end of the knife.

2. Turn the strips horizontally, and cut into cubes using the low or high technique, whichever is more comfortable.

SLICING A BONELESS ROAST

Simply stated, this is the classic high technique (page 90) using a carving (possibly Granton-edge) or a 10-inch scalloped-edge knife in the perpendicular position. This technique is no different than cutting fruits or vegetables using the high technique. Most people get into trouble slicing a roast because the first motion with the knife is down, not across. Depending on the thickness of the roast, two or maybe even three passes will be needed. The knife must be kept angled until the slice is nearly separated, then the blade is leveled when it reaches the board. The cutting is done on the push only; the knife is kept in the groove and repositioned on the pull.

FISH AND SHELLFISH FABRICATION

Fabricating your own fish and shellfish involves an investment in some unique knives and in practice time, but it is an exciting challenge. I am a proponent of cooking fish whole whenever possible—a practice employed and enjoyed by many cultures around the world—but I do enjoy sautéed, pan-fried, and even deep-fried fillets.

Don't buy fillets unless you have no choice. If your fishmonger sells whole fish, ask for it to be filleted while you wait. Get to know your fishmonger and make it clear that you only want quality products—I expect mine to tell me if what I have ordered is not up to my standards and steer me toward something else.

If the fish you are contemplating has not yet been gutted, look for clear and bright rather than sunken eyes, and tight scales. Ask to see the gills—the redder, the better. Although you are walking away with the fillets, you have actually paid for the whole fish and are entitled to the frame or skeleton of the fish that's left after gutting and filleting. When you have become a regular customer you can ask your fishmonger to save four or five frames for you to use in fish stock. Generally you'll want the frames of white-meat fish only. Dark-meat fish such as mackerel or bluefish will produce a stock with a strong, oily flavor not suitable for neutral stocks. Every fish market knows how many fish they are going to fillet or keep whole. If you don't request them, the frames will be thrown out.

Tell your fishmonger to gut but not scale your fish, unless you want to cook the fish whole, in which case you should have it gutted and scaled. Unless you can scale fish in the great outdoors, have the fishmonger do it for you or you will be picking scales off the floor, walls, and ceiling for days.

Two types of fish—flatfish and round fish—will be used to illustrate the filleting techniques. Each type has a different skeletal structure and requires different knives.

Flatfish

This category of fish includes flounder, Dover sole, turbot, and halibut. Flatfish are dark on top and have a lighter underbelly. They swim horizontally at or near the bottom, dark-side up, so as to be nearly invisible to predators. Most of the species mentioned above are small ($1\frac{1}{2}$ to 6 pounds), but halibut can be as long as 10 feet and weigh a much as 600 pounds.

Newly hatched flatfish are bilaterally symmetrical but soon thereafter the body flattens and one eye migrates so that both eyes are on top of the head. Long rib bones radiate from the backbone toward the dorsal and anal fins on each side, with thinner bones supporting the fins. The back and rib bones will help to guide the knife as you fillet.

Filleting Flatfish

For filleting flatfish, I use a 6-inch semiflexible filleting knife. The fishmonger has removed all visible viscera (guts). The resulting cavity is called the visceral cavity.

1. Place the fish on the board, dark-side up, with the head facing away from you. Locate the visceral cavity and the thin, center line that runs from head to tail just above the backbone.

2. Make a diagonal cut just behind the cavity, all across the body.

3. Cut down the center line from head to tail. You should feel the tip of the knife on the backbone.

4. Make a horizontal cut just above the tail.

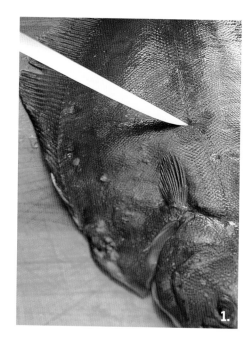

Right-handed chefs will work on the left side first; lefties will reverse this.

5. At the top of the left-side fillet, insert about 1 1/2 inches of the tip of the knife underneath the fillet and on the backbone.

6. With the flat of the knife against the rib bones, make a series of short, overlapping, pulled strokes, working from head to tail, pulling the fillet to the side as you go. Often, the fillet cannot be removed in one sweep down the ribs. Halfway across the ribs, go back to the top and repeat the overlapping-pulling motions again.

7. Fold the fillet back into place. Turn the fish so that the head is now facing you and repeat the process starting at the tail.

8. Fold this fillet back into place. Turn the fish over and use the same techniques on the light side. Keeping the thicker, dark-side fillets on while you remove the fillets from the light side makes removal of these thinner fillets easier.

9. To remove the fillet, either make a head-to-tail cut where the fillet ends and the small bones that support the dorsal and anal fins begin, or cut past the small bones, pull the fillet off, and trim away the bones. Turn the fish over and remove the thicker fillets. When both fillets have been removed, the skeletal structure is revealed.

This technique yields four fillets—two thick and two thin. It is possible to remove the top and bottom fillets in one piece by making a cut down the length of one side where the fillet ends and carefully working the knife toward then over the center bone, continuing on the other side. Use the bones as your guide and make gentle, overlapping, pulling cuts.

Skinning a Fillet

1. Place the fillet skin-side down at the edge of your cutting board with the knife at a right angle. Keep the knife's handle behind the board at all times. Hold on to the tail section with thumb and index finger and insert the knife as best you can between the meat and the skin. You will lose about $1/2$ inch or so.

2. Keep the knife against the skin and raise the spine just high enough to scrape along the skin but not cut it. Make long, zigzag scrapes from tail to head. This technique is very similar to the parallel zigzag motion used to make horizontal cuts through an onion except that when skinning a fillet the knife is turned in the opposite direction and the blade is angled slightly down. Pull the skin slightly down and away from the knife as you go.

3. The properly executed skinning technique leaves no skin on the flesh. If the scales had been removed, the skin would be so thin that it would most likely tear. If you plan to leave the skin on, have your fishmonger scale it for you.

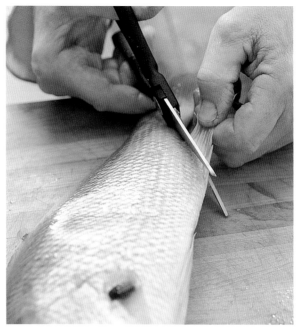

Round Fish

When they hear the word *fish*, most people think of a round fish, a water creature that swims vertically with eyes on both sides of its head. It has only two fillets, one on each side. The skeleton is usually not as symmetrical as that of flatfish; the dorsal (top) bones are longer than the ribs that extend from the backbone to the belly. The backbone, as with the flat fish, runs down the center from head to tail and serves as a guide for the knife.

Use a pair of sturdy kitchen scissors to remove the fins, especially the sharp dorsal (top) one, if your fishmongers has not already done so. In round fish, the visceral cavity is in the center of the body, so the gill cover, that almost shell-like flap you lifted to inspect the gills for color, will be your starting point.

For filleting round fish, I use an 8-inch fillet knife instead of the 6-inch one used for the flatfish so that I don't have to switch knives to remove the skin—the round fish fillet is wider than the flatfish fillet.

Filleting Round Fish

1. Place the fish at the near edge of your board, dorsal side facing you, the head toward your knife-hand side. Angle the knife toward the head and cut into the flesh just behind the gill cover until you feel the backbone.

2. Turn the blade up and cut the belly flap.

3. Insert $1\frac{1}{2}$ to 2 inches of the knife at and under the top of the fillet and against the backbone. Make short overlapping strokes towards the tail, pulling the fillet aside as you go.

4. Near the tail, push the knife across the bone to the other side and loosen the meat at the tail.

5. Go back to the top and work the fillet off the bones.

6. Turn the fish so the dorsal side faces you, the head toward your holding-hand side. For the first cut behind the gill cover, angle the knife toward the head and cut into the flesh until you reach the backbone.

7. Turn the blade up and cut the belly flap. Then turn the blade towards the tail, knife turned outwards to make the overlapping cuts. After you have loosened the tail section, turn the knife towards your holding hand and work it from tail to head to remove the fillet.

Skinning a Round Fish

1. Place the fillet skin-side down at the edge of your cutting board with the knife at a right angle. Keep the knife's handle behind the board at all times. Hold on to the tail section with thumb and index finger and insert the knife as best you can between the meat and the skin. You will lose about $1/2$ inch or so.

2. Keep the knife against the skin and raise the spine just high enough to scrape along the skin but not cut it. Make long, zigzag scrapes from tail to head. This technique is very similar to the parallel zigzag motion used to make horizontal cuts through an onion except that when skinning a fillet the knife is turned in the opposite direction and the blade is angled slightly down. Pull the skin slightly down and away from the knife as you go.

3. The properly executed skinning technique leaves no skin on the flesh.

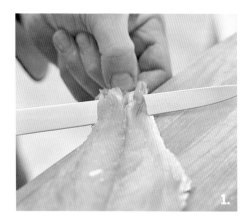

Salmon

If the salmon at my Brooklyn market are in the 4-to-6 pound range, I like to fillet them myself, but I let the dealer do the bigger fish since he has a much longer counter. I use a 10-inch, sharp-tipped carving knife for filleting the salmon, not a so-called salmon slicer, a thin and very flexible blade used to cut paper-thin slices from smoked salmon.

The placement of the fish and the first steps in removing the fillets are similar to those shown for the snapper:

1. Make an angled cut behind the gill cover down to the backbone.

2. Turn the blade up and cut the belly flap.

3. Insert 2 to 3 inches of the knife at and under the top of the fillet and against the backbone.

4. Then lift the belly flap and push the knife across the backbone to the other side.

5. Keep the belly flap lifted and, with the knife's edge on the backbone, zigzag to and through the tail section where the fillet is removed.

6. Turn the fish to remove side two. The sequence of cuts remains the same. The fillet is removed at the tail. The knife will be turned away from your holding hand.

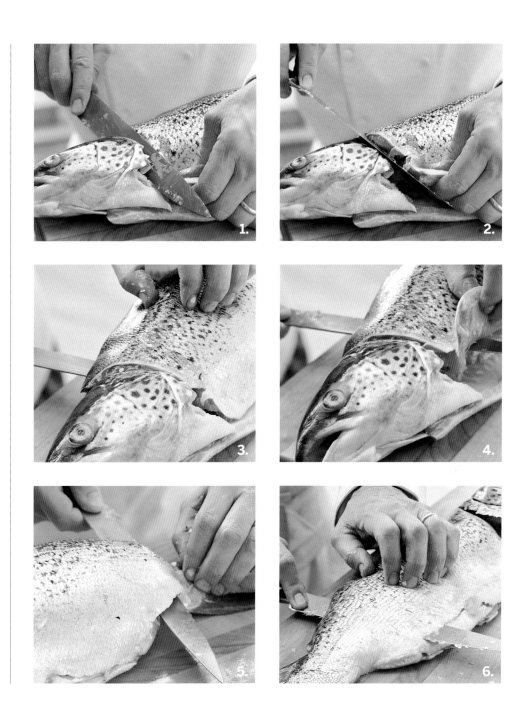

7. If any rib bones remain on the fillet, insert the knife underneath where the backbone used to be. Keep the knife angled up against the ribs and remove them, along with any fatty material, at the belly.

8. The skinning process is the same as for flatfish and round fish.

9. Those little white bones you see near the center are called pinbones, and they need to be removed. Run your fingers across them to loosen the tops, then remove with needle-nose pliers.

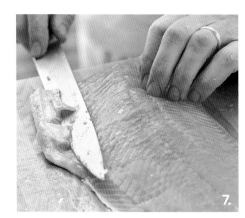

Shrimp

Those of you who think you are buying fresh shrimp at the market are in for a rude awakening. Fresh shrimp are rarely available to the general public unless you live in a shrimp-producing area of the United States, such as on the Gulf Coast. Most of the shrimp available in the fish markets have been frozen and packaged in 5-pound blocks. The best-quality frozen shrimp come from freezer boats, large freighterlike ships that haul in, sort, and freeze the catch on board.

Shrimp are sold by the count per pound. Designations such as U-12 (up to 12), 21–25 and 41–50 indicate the number of shrimp per pound. The higher the number, the smaller the shrimp. Depending on the waters from which they are hauled, the shell can be gray, light brown, pink or, in the case of the Asian tiger shrimp, lined with dark stripes. Avoid shrimp that have a strong ammonia smell or dark spots on the shells.

The vein is actually the intestinal tract of the shrimp and runs down the back. Most of the time I cook shelled, medium shrimp without bothering to devein them. The vein is not harmful to eat, just unsightly. I have eaten vein-in shrimp for over forty years, especially in New York's Asian restaurants where shrimp can be served with the head and in the shell. I devein shrimp when cooking the larger sizes or anytime the shrimp are going to be either partially opened or butterflied.

Peeling, Deveining, and Butterflying Shrimp

KNIFE: 5-INCH BONING KNIFE OR 6-INCH UTILITY KNIFE

To peel the shrimp, pull off the legs and use your thumbs to remove the shell. For a nicer presentation, you can leave the last segment and tail on. You can freeze the shells and use them to make a seafood stock.

1. To devein the shrimp, either hold it in your hand, vein-side (back) up, and make a pulled ¼-inch incision from head to tail (or last segment), or place the shrimp on the board and make the incision with the back facing you.

2. Remove the vein with the tip of the knife and place it on a paper towel. Someone may try to sell you a special knife or plastic gizmo for removing shrimp veins when a paring, utility, or 5-inch boning knife (as shown right) will do rather well. I belong to the "fewer gadgets is better" school.

3. Keep the tail segment attached. Place the shrimp on the board and make a parallel, pulled cut from the tail segment to the head, cutting almost through to the bottom.

4. Spread the two halves open like a book using the flat of the knife to press.

4B.

BIBLIOGRAPHY OF BOOKS AND WEBSITES

Books:

Beard, James, et al., editors. *The Cook's Catalogue*. New York: Avon, 1975.

Bridge, Fred, and Jean F. Tibbetts. *The Well-Tooled Kitchen*. New York: William Morrow, 1991.

Campbell, Susan. *Cook's Tools*. New York: Bantam, 1981.

Child, Julia. *The Way To Cook*. New York: Alfred A. Knopf, 1989.

Conran, Terence and Caroline. *The Cook Book*. New York: Crown, 1980.

The Culinary Institute of America. *The Professional Chef's Knife Kit*. New York: John Wiley & Sons, 2000.

Day, Christopher P., with Brenda R. Carlos. *Knife Skills for Chefs.* Upper Saddle River, NJ: Pearson Prentice Hall, 2007.

Gisslen, Wayne. *Professional Cooking*, 4th edition. New York: John Wiley & Sons, 1999.

Pépin, Jacques. *La Méthode*. New York: Times Books, 1979.

Pépin, Jacques. *La Technique*. New York: Times Books, 1976.

Victorinox. *The Knife and Its History*. Ibach, Germany: 1984.

Willan, Anne. *LaVarenne Practique*. New York: Crown, 1989.

Useful Websites:

If there is no major cookware store in your immediate area, the following websites will offer you an opportunity to do some comparison shopping for knives, cutting boards, honing and sharpening equipment. Observe the return policy and shipping charges carefully.

www.broadwaypanhandler.com

www.cookswares.com

www.chefdepot.net

www.chefknifes.com

www.chefknivestogo.com

www.cutlery.com

www.cutleryandmore.com

www.fantes.com

www.jbprince.com

www.kitchencutlery.net

www.knife-depot.com

www.knifeoutlet.com

www.knifemerchant.com

www.korin.com

www.nwcutlery.com

www.surlatable.com

www.thebestthings.com/knives

www.williams-sonoma.com

Maintenance—Where to get your knives sharpened

The following sites have information on how to bring or mail your knives in to have them sharpened:

www.accuratesharp.com – Tempe, AZ

www.ambrosicutlery.com – Mahopac, NY

www.broadwaypanhandler.com – New York, NY

www.countryknives.com – Intercourse, PA

www.holleyknives.com mail-in only

www.jivano's.com – San Francisco

kramerknives.com – Olympia, WA

www.mrleonardknifesharpener.com – Midlothian, VA

www.mortysknives.com – Long Island, NY

www.northbeachshop.com – San Francisco

www.razorsharpcutlery – San Francisco

www.theknifeguy.com – mail-in only

Caveat Emptor:

Many of the larger retail stores offer a knife sharpening service. Please read the cautions in the chapter on sharpening. Know what you brought or sent in. Know what you got back.

ACKNOWLEDGMENTS

This book would not have come to fruition without the complete dedication of:

Michael Bourret, my agent at Dystel & Goderich who taught me to be patient; Marisa Bulzone, the acquisition editor; and Luisa Weiss, the book's editor and shepherdess. Special kudos go to the designer, LeAnna Weller Smith; the production manager, Tina Cameron; the photographer, Mark Thomas, without whom this book would be but a lot of words; and Alan Madison, the director of the DVD that accompanies the book.

Special thanks to Rick Smilow and the staff of The Institute of Culinary Education for their support of my Knife Skills classes and this book; Cathy McCauley and Al Cappellini of Cooktique; David Martone of Classic Thyme; Kings' Supermarkets; Sur La Table; Bill Liederman, who gave me my start at The New School Culinary Arts Program; and all the other cooking schools that have afforded me the opportunity to hone my craft.

I am extremely grateful to the following individuals or companies for their assistance with product or invaluable technical information without which this book could not have been written:

Cutting Boards:

J. K. Adams Co., Bally Block Co., John Boos & Co., Al Ladd Woodworking, Michigan Maple Block Co., Snow River Wood Products, The Vermont Butcher Block and Board Co., and Totally Bamboo.

Knife Manufacturers:

Dexter-Russell, Inc., F. Dick, Edgecraft Corporation, Granton, Zwilling J. A. Henckels, Kershaw Knives, Korin Japanese Trading, Lamson and Goodnow, Messermeister, Sabatier, Swiss Army/Victorinox, and a special thanks to the Wüsthof-Trident of America (and Germany) organization for its many years of support.

Other Companies or Organizations:

Broadway Panhandler, The Holley Manufacturing Co., JB Prince, Julius Kirschner and Sons, EDACO, Knifemerchant, Morty The Knife Man, The National Onion Association, and Norton-Pike.

Finally, I wish to thank the thousands of students who have allowed me to share my ideas and helped me to become a better teacher.

INDEX

(Page numbers in *italic* refer to illustrations.)